HAREWOOD

— YORKSHIRE —

— A GUIDE —

"I would not exceed the limits of expense that I hav[e]
Let us do everything properly and well, ma[...]

Edwin Lascelles to Robert Adam

HAREWOOD HOUSE TRUST

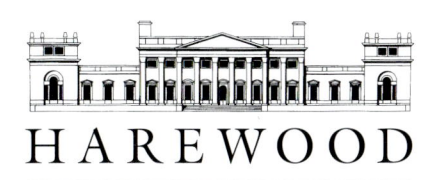

HAREWOOD

Introduction

It is well over 200 years since my family built this House and we have lived in all or part of it ever since. A few years ago we formed a Trust to assume responsibility for running it, and the Trust now undertakes the work of renovation and maintenance with money it gets from an endowment as well as from the visitors who come to Harewood.

Those are the two main sources of revenue to meet the very considerable costs of maintaining a house built long ago and therefore constantly in need of repair – the entire roof had to be replaced during the winter of 1993-4. We have recently started to receive grants from public bodies like English Heritage and the EEC – our first such grant came in 1994 for the roof and for the very expensive work on the restoration of the Terrace – but the bulk of the Trust's income is self-generated.

Extensive work on the interior of the House has been going on since the middle 1980s, and this Guide Book has consequently been thoroughly revised. My hope is that it draws the visitor's attention to what will interest him or her most on the way round – that probably means what interests me most. Earlier books on Harewood, as well as guide books and articles, have been ruthlessly pillaged in an effort to find the information which will be most useful to the visitor. Above all, I am grateful to my friend Richard Buckle, from whom I have (with his generous permission) quoted extensively (sometimes, as he well knows, without specific acknowledgement). Other hands have written areas where particular expertise, or a particular emphasis, seemed appropriate, but most of this Guide Book is written (or pirated) by me.

All of us responsible for this House are delighted you have come. We hope you enjoy your visit, that you will come again, and that between us we can keep Harewood alive, not just for members of the Lascelles family but for future generations of visitors as well.

History of Harewood

Above: The Castle in decay about 1800; from an old print.

Below: Gawthorpe Hall about 1720. Note the church, top right, and Almscliff, top left.

At the time of the Norman Conquest in 1066, Harewood as recorded in the Domesday Book seems to have belonged to Tor, Sprot and Grim, three Saxon Chieftains, who as supporters of Earl Morcar were dispossessed by the new King, their lands passing into his domain. During the reign of William I, Harewood with other large estates in Yorkshire went to Robert de Romelli, a Norman nobleman. Early in the next century the Castle, standing no more than half a mile to the south of the River Wharfe, was built to guard a ford in the river against marauders from the north, and by 1209 Harewood was a prosperous market town with its first charter.

Through female inheritance the Castle and Estate passed through various hands until in 1365 it was bought by Sir William Aldburgh, who was messenger to Edward Balliol, Edward I's nominee as King of Scotland. When Balliol was driven from Scotland, he is said to have taken refuge in Harewood Castle, and his arms together with those of Aldburgh are still to be seen on the ruined walls. Sir William Aldburgh had two daughters, one married to Sir Richard Redmayne and the other to Sir William Ryther; as co-heiresses at his death, they shared the estate, the families taking it in turn to live at the Castle. The Gascoigne family, connected by marriage with both Redmaynes and Rythers, were living at neighbouring Gawthorpe when they added Harewood to their domains.

In 1580 the estate passed to the Wentworths but the son of the ill-fated Earl of Strafford, who lived at Gawthorpe and was beheaded under Charles I for treason, sold it in 1657 to Sir John Cutler, satirised (some say unjustly) by Pope in his Moral Essays:

Cutler saw tenants break and houses fall
For very want, he could not build a wall.
His only daughter in a stranger's power
For very want, he could not pay a dower.

From the Conquest until it was acquired by Cutler, a period of almost 600 years, the estate passed by descent, varied only by marriage, sometimes through the female line.

In 1738, it was bought from a certain John Boulter by Henry Lascelles of Northallerton, and for more than two and a half centuries has remained in his family's possession.

Harewood and the Lascelles family

A Lascelles travelled with William the Conqueror and is mentioned in Domesday, and the family has certainly lived in Yorkshire since 1315, when John de Lascelles lived in the North Riding at Hinderskelfe, now called Castle Howard. The family moved to Northallerton, and Francis Lascelles was Colonel in the Parliamentary Army and later Member of Parliament (1653) for the North Riding of Yorkshire, a tradition carried on by many of his descendants over 200 years. His grandson bought Gawthorpe and Harewood, and his great-grandson Edwin made the decision to build a new house on top of the hill.

By the late seventeenth century, the family's connection with Barbados and the sugar plantations they acquired there was firmly established, and Edwin was born there, as was his cousin, Edward Lascelles, who eventually inherited his estates from Edwin and was made the first Earl of Harewood. It was the Barbados connection and the increase in the family fortunes which made possible the building of Harewood (my family only relinquished its links with Barbados in the 1970s).

Edwin Lascelles was quite clearly a difficult customer with what is euphemistically known as a mind of his own. He was over forty when his father died and immediately set about realising the plans which must have been maturing in his mind for years. After rejecting plans submitted by William Chambers, he commissioned **John Carr** of York to design the house. Carr's work at Harewood was extensive, starting with the Stables (between the House and the Lake),

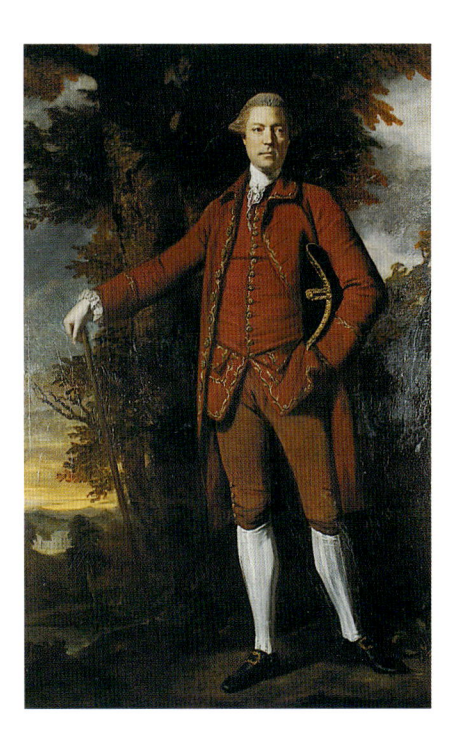

*Above: Reynolds's portrait of **Edwin Lascelles**, who inherited a manor house, spent carefully and left a mansion.*

Below: Carr's front elevation for Harewood (from 'Vitruvius Britannicus').

*Above: **Robert Adam** by George Willison (National Portrait Gallery).*

*Below right: **John Carr** by William Beechey (National Portrait Gallery).*

and continuing with House, Farm and the 'model' village which now stands to the East of the Leeds-Harrogate road. Plans for the new house were drawn up within three years of the death of Edwin's father, and in 1758, while Carr was working on the Stable block, Edwin showed the plans to **Robert Adam**, the 33-year-old Scottish architect who was in the process of establishing himself in London after three years of intensive study in Italy. Adam favoured a neo-classical style lighter than the Palladian whose main English proponent was Chambers, but he found little to alter in Carr's plans. Nonetheless, he wrote to his brother James: "I have thrown in large, semi-circular back courts with columns betwixt the house and the wings." James replied: "It affords me the greatest pleasure that you have tickled it up so as to dazzle the eyes of the squire." Not much remains of Adam's architectural alterations: Edwin rejected one of the courts and the Victorians did away with the other.

Edwin's steward was Samuel Popplewell, responsible for general management of the estate (we should now call him 'agent'), but he seems to have had a hard time with his master, who wrote: "When I have no reason to complain, I shall ... desist making use of harsh expressions and there I desire you would not pretend to tell me how I am to write to you ... I presume to be as good judge of the management of my affairs as you, and if I am conscious of a great expense, and what done for it doth not appear adequate, who hath a better right to find fault than myself. I think they have been too hasty in beginning to build." And to Adam, more temperately but just as firmly: "I would not exceed the limits of expense that I have always set myself. Let us do everything properly and well, *mais pas trop*."

If Adam's effect on the exterior of the House was limited, he seems to have had something like a free hand in the interior and, in spite of some later alterations, it remains one of his great achievements. His hand can be seen everywhere, whether in ceilings or carpets, in elaborate decoration on almost any flat surface, or in the choice of Joseph Rose and William Collins for the plasterwork, of Angelica Kaufmann, Antonio Zucchi and Biagio Rebecca to paint the decorative panels on ceilings and walls, or – most important of all – of Thomas Chippendale to supply the furniture. Adam's is the controlling mind, but I suppose it would only be fair in assessing the results to bracket his flair and taste with the sense of proportion, imagination and indomitable will of Edwin who set it all in motion.

The foundation stone of Harewood was laid in January 1759, Adam's decorative schemes date from 1765, the house became habitable in 1771 (when Gawthorpe was pulled down), and the Gallery, its grandest room, was finished in 1772. The same year, **Lancelot 'Capability' Brown**, the most renowned designer of English landscape (himself also an architect), submitted plans for the Park, surrounding the Lake with plantations and gently undulating parkland where before had been fields and pasture. (Edwin by damming the stream had already created the Lake.) For nine years, Lancelot Brown worked on the Park and he was paid a total of over £6,000, a big sum in those days but perhaps not too much for what the writer Dorothy Stroud in her book about him called "one of the most delectable of landscapes". What he liked to do was not to design gardens in geometrical shapes enclosed in meticulously clipped hedges but rather to point up the possibilities of nature, by regulating the natural curves of the ground (hundreds of men were employed to shift earth from one place to another), and by judicious planting. Humphry Repton, architect and landscape designer, was called in (1800-02), and added some ideas, but time, which fells even the mightiest of trees, and wind, which can destroy whole acres of planting, (we lost 10,000 mature and 20,000 young trees in two days of gale in 1962), inevitably affect plans like Brown's and Repton's. Nonetheless, most of what they shaped and planted and a good deal of what they aimed for is still in working order at Harewood.

Thomas Chippendale, born a few miles away at Otley in 1718, worked at Harewood from 1767 and was responsible for the furniture and furnishings throughout the House. He had emigrated to London and the commission, one of his most elaborate, was fulfilled from his workshop in St. Martin's Lane. Though he necessarily started to work within a style which has been categorised as rococo (without the overtones of excess that

Top left: **Lancelot 'Capability' Brown** *by Nathaniel Dance* (National Portrait Gallery).

Top right: **Harewood from the South**, *by J.M.W. Turner (1798).*

Above: View of the House from the south today (1994).

Richmond's portrait of Louisa, Lady Harewood, who reconstructed the House.

One of Sir Charles Barry's versions of a new North elevation for Louisa's replanned house (compare Malton's 1788 view, opposite).

word sometimes implies), he was later much influenced by Adam. He brought the design of English furniture to new levels of sophistication and indeed of perfection so that, perhaps for the first time, what was made in this country rivalled the more elaborate products of France, and his best furniture possesses a simplicity of line, almost a chastity, which is hard to find in its French equivalents.

Edwin Lascelles built the House, so his effect on what we see today is the strongest of any of Harewood's owners. Edward, his cousin and heir, added to the collection of portraits and in 1812 became the 1st Earl of Harewood. His eldest son, **Edward, Viscount Lascelles**, who died before his father, was an active patron of the arts, a friend of Turner and Girtin as well as himself a capable draughtsman. He brought together the collection of Chinese celadon and French porcelain as well as commissioning paintings from the leading practitioners of the day. His brother Henry succeeded as 2nd Earl, and Henry's son, also Henry, after fighting at Waterloo, married Louisa Thynne, who not only needed a bigger house for their family of thirteen children and for entertaining, but may additionally have had ancestral longings for the palatial proportions of her family home, Longleat.

Louisa called in Sir Charles Barry, the architect of the Houses of Parliament, who gave the house a third storey, swept away the classical portico on the south façade and added the massive Terrace which transformed the Georgian country house into something like an Italian palazzo. The early Victorians were no respecters of the past and the positive nature of their taste resulted at Harewood in alterations inside the house as well as to its exterior. Rooms changed shape as well as use, passages were introduced where none had existed, Adam's decoration underwent subtle (and not so subtle) change, and at least three rooms were substantially re-modelled, not always (one may now think) for the better. On the other hand, there is no doubt that the House owes its present heroic character to the terrace Barry and Louisa added on the south.

The most positive thing the 4th Earl did for Harewood was to marry the grand-daughter of the Prime Minister **George Canning** and niece of Lord Canning, (Viceroy of India at the time of the Mutiny and nicknamed 'Clemency' Canning because people in England disapproved of his less than draconian punishment of the mutineers). In 1917, sixty-three years after Elizabeth de Burgh's death, her brother, 2nd **Marquess of Clanricarde**, died leaving everything he possessed, not to his nephew, whom he disliked and who was the 5th Earl of Harewood, but rather to my father, whom he had met in his club when he was home on leave from France. My father thus became heir to Canning papers, books and pictures which are at Harewood to this day.

My father was **Henry, 6th Earl of Harewood**, and he used considerable portions of his Clanricarde inheritance to buy Italian pictures, so that an arts writer recently described him as one of the last collectors in the English tradition of the Grand Tour and bracketed him with the Prince Consort in the nineteenth century. Later he and my mother, Princess Mary, The Princess Royal*, embarked on the work of restoration which we in this generation have attempted to carry forward. Between 1929, when my grandfather died after 37 years at Harewood, and 1939, when the last war began, rooms were refurbished and pictures throughout the house re-hung so that for the first time for a century Adam's schemes re-emerged as the dominating influence, Chippendale's sets of furniture were re-upholstered and reunited, and the house regained the condition its begetters must have planned. At that point the war intervened and the house again served, as it had between 1914 and 1918, as a convalescent hospital.

Almost as soon as it was built, Harewood became of interest to sightseers, visitors were taken round by arrangement with the house-keeper, a guide book was published early in the nineteenth century, and the place was of sufficient fame to be painted on an ice pail made by Wedgwood for Catherine the Great of Russia. In spite of sales of pictures, furniture, plate, books and china, made necessary by heavy death duties in 1947, the house is still full of treasures, and since my family have retreated to manageable flats on the top floor there are more rooms open to the public and consequently more works of art on display than ever before.

Roger Fenton's well-known photograph of the South view from the house, 1860.

* *The title 'The Princess Royal', belongs to the eldest daughter of the sovereign, but is not automatically inherited, rather bestowed at discretion. My mother was awarded it in 1932, a year after the death of the previous holder, her aunt, Princess Louise, Duchess of Fife.*

*Thomas Malton: **The North façade**, 1788.*

Castle, Church and Village

The **Castle** stands at the extreme north of the village near the main road on a ridge in the midst of woods. It was built about the middle of the twelfth century by Robert de Lisle. A more precise date, 1116, is given for the foundation of the Church by William de Curcy, husband of Avicia de Romelli, to whose father the estate was given by William the Conqueror, the first of several examples of Harewood passing through the female line. In spite of dilapidation, the Castle's twin towers are still visible today as you drive along the Harrogate road, and have provided romantic subject matter for painters over the years. In the mid-seventeenth century, in Strafford ownership, it seems to have been abandoned and rapidly became a ruin, subsequently serving as a reservoir of stone for the village.

Alabaster tomb of Lord Chief Justice Gascoigne in the Church.

Harewood Castle by J.M.W. Turner.

In the early fifteenth century, the original pre-Norman **Church** was rebuilt for the grand-daughters of Sir William Aldburgh, and in the 1760s it underwent considerable alterations at the hands of Edwin Lascelles. A hundred years later, the interior was extensively Victorianised, the old glass replaced, a wooden roof substituted for the 18th century plasterwork, and a new altar, font, pulpit and lectern provided. The Church flourished until the late 1960s when the congregation became less and less willing to walk the half mile from the village and, after the death of the Vicar, Canon H.H. Griffith, incumbent at Harewood for some forty years, it was declared redundant.

What sounds like the end was in fact something of a new beginning as the Redundant Churches Fund embarked on an ambitious programme of restoration of the splendid mediaeval monuments to members of the Redman, Ryther and Gascoigne families, all former owners of Harewood, the largest and finest collection in any English church other than a cathedral and rivalled in

All Saints Church, Harewood.

Yorkshire only by the monuments at Methley. These alabaster carvings are among the great treasures of Harewood and they include, in the south transept, a commemoration of the former Lord Chief Justice Gascoigne who, among other feats of judicial daring, refused to try Archbishop Scrope for treason and sent Prince Hal, the future King Henry V, to prison for complicity in robbery.

The village probably reached its high point in the early thirteenth century when it was granted a charter; in 1570, James Ryther wrote to Lord Burghley, the great statesman of Queen Elizabeth's time: "Harwood [then spelt without an 'e'] is a great thoroughfare town from Lancashire and the west countries to Yorkshire". In 1753 there were riots arising out of opposition to the turnpike near Harewood Bridge, and men were arrested after a fight nearby which escalated a day or two later until, after the Riot Act had been read, a pitched battle took place in Briggate in Leeds between dragoons from York and the mob, which ended with eight dead and fifty wounded.

At one time there were no fewer than six public houses in the village, but Edwin Lascelles rebuilt it as a model village (see the watercolour by Varley which shows the process half complete and as seen from an Eastern vantage point) and an attempt was made to establish a ribbon manufactory, but this was ended after a few years. About a hundred years later, Jones in his *History of Harewood* refers to the twenty-two stage coaches which passed through the village every day until the advent of railroads. Another century further on, village life as elsewhere has become less self-sufficient and more reliant on the city, so that with increased mechanisation and the decline of agriculture, the problem is to retain any character beyond that of a dormitory for Leeds.

John Varley: The start of building the 'model' village, planned by Edwin Lascelles and designed by John Carr.

11

The Entrance Hall

The eight beechwood chairs are fine examples of a design which, slightly varied, is to be found in the halls of many houses for which Chippendale provided furniture. Their purpose is to decorate, not to be sat on.

*Below: Bas-relief by William Collins: **The Chariot of Phaeton.***

The halls of houses Adam designed tend towards the heroic and Harewood is no exception; indeed, says Richard Buckle, it "has a stern character, as if it were a place from which to see heroes off to war" – witness the 'engaged' columns which seem to refer back to an earlier architectural age. At Harewood, Adam designed the ceilings, friezes and chimneypieces throughout the house, and his habit was to aim at an overall decorative scheme with everything part of a unified design. (In the Hall for instance the ox skulls, a feature of the frieze, recur over the doors and on the chimneypiece carved in marble). He outlined his schemes in some detail but left their realisation to the stuccoists, Joseph Rose of York and William Collins, whose own fantasy was engaged to some purpose – the wedding of Neptune and Amphitrite is the subject of the oblong relief over the fireplace with the Chariot of Phaeton opposite, where was once a second fireplace.

As Adam conceived it, the Hall was a noble ante-chamber rather than a place in which to linger, but the inventory made in 1795 suggests that 25 years after the House was first occupied it was already used as something like an extra sitting room. Certainly that was how the Victorians employed it – can you wonder, with thirteen children? – and by the end of the century photographs show it heavily furnished, the plaster statues from the antique replaced in the niches by busts on pedestals, with palms in pots on either side of the internal door and antlers flanking the fireplace.

We have tried a measure of restoration: the columns painted to imitate porphyry marble (as described in Jewell's Guide Book of 1819; the painting almost certainly *not* part of Adam's scheme but a later addition); the chairs stripped of their later varnish and painted (as Chippendale suggests) to suit the colours of the room; and we plan to restore statues to take the place of the Victorian busts (which will be placed elsewhere in the house).

On either side of the door into the Library stand a pair of **Famille Verte Vases** made in about 1690 in China. Emblazoned with the arms of Miguel d'Almeida, Captain General of the Portuguese East Indies, after

Chinese 'famille verte' vases dating from c.1690.

the relief of Lucknow during the Indian Mutiny they were presented to Lady Canning, wife of the Governor General, by General Outram and the garrison who owed their rescue "to the orders and exertions of the noble Earl, her husband".

The whole space is now dominated by the most important twentieth century addition to the collection, *Jacob Epstein's* **Adam**, a carving made in 1938-9 from a pillar of alabaster and brought to Harewood in the 1960s. It represents not so much the architect Edwin Lascelles called in to polish up the house he was building (as some visitors have surmised), rather the progenitor of us all, striving here for the survival of what he has engendered. The degree to which Epstein's Adam fits into Robert Adam's overall decorative scheme may intrigue the visitor.

Adam's face gazing upwards at some of his namesake's work.

13

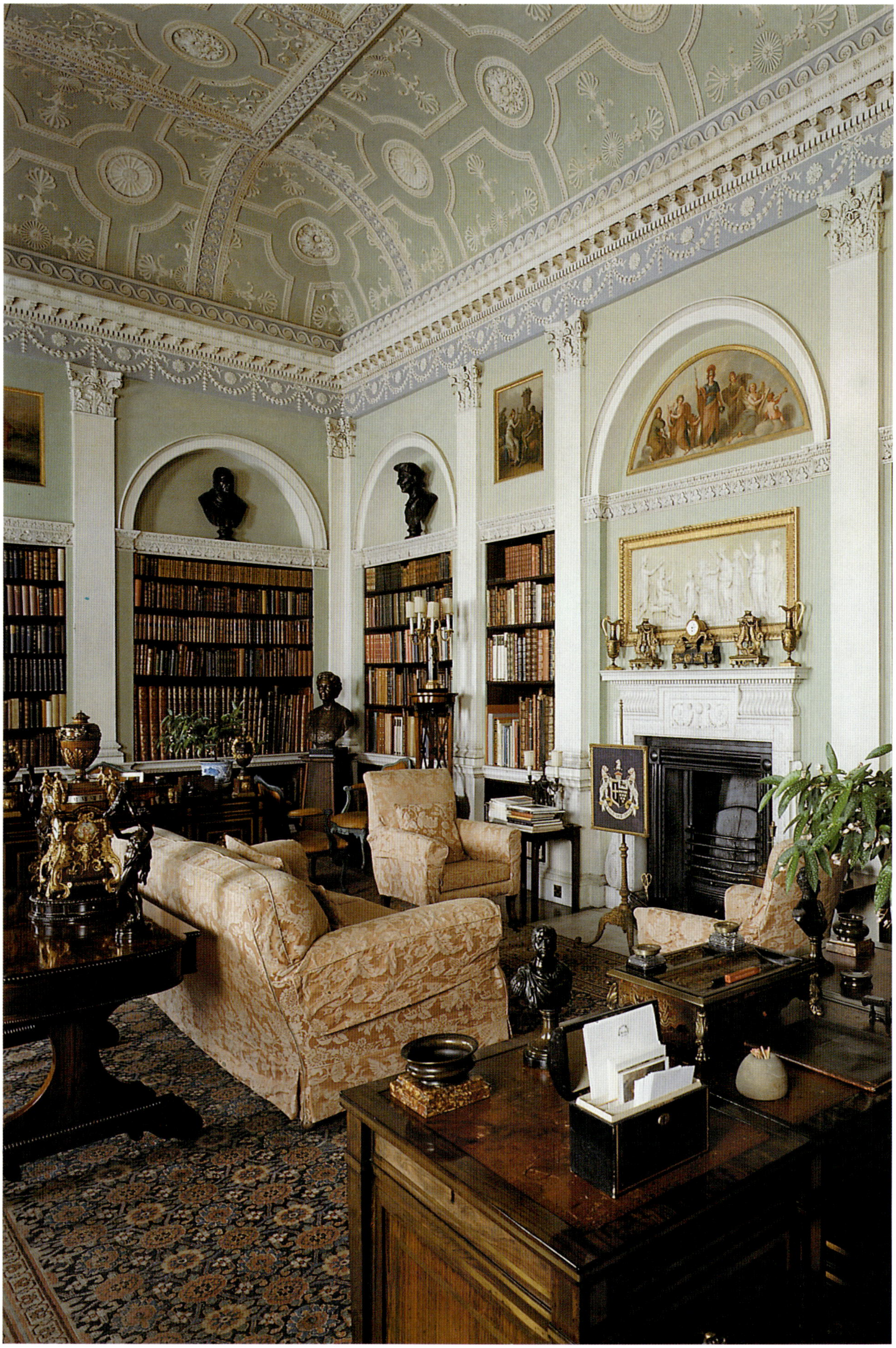

The Old Library

To move from the pomp of Adam's Hall to the comfort of the Old Library (*Old* in the sense of *original,* to distinguish it from the larger room converted to its present function by Sir Charles Barry and to be seen later) is to exchange the formal for the domestic. Corinthian pilasters divide up the room, whose ceiling and walls have been repainted using what scraping the later over-painting revealed as Adam's original colour scheme – basically, green and white, with the frieze in contrasting grey. The ceiling is a typically elaborate, well-balanced Adam design, one of many to be seen throughout the House.

The eight Chippendale chairs were made for this room in the early 1770s. Above the bookcases and over the fireplace are paintings by *Biagio Rebecca* (see panel below). The room also contains a fine late eighteenth century clock by *Allen,* with a dial revolving round the top; and a posthumous bust of my mother, Her Royal Highness Princess Mary (whose home Harewood was from 1929 until her death in 1965) by F.E.McWilliam (1909-1992).

Bronze bust of Mary, The Princess Royal, by F. E. McWilliam.

Detail of a fine late 18th century clock by Allen.

Three decorative painters who worked with Adam at Harewood

Biagio Rebecca (1735-1808) was of Italian descent but lived and worked in England. Became an A.R.A. in 1771, worked at Windsor Castle, Somerset House, Audley End, Kedleston, and specialised in the imitation of antique bas-relief, such as the example over the chimneypiece here. The pictures in the Gallery ceiling are also by him.

Angelica Kaufmann (1741-1807) was born in Switzerland and became known as a youthful prodigy in Italy. Brought to England in 1765, she became in 1768 one of the thirty-six founder members of the Royal Academy. Sir Joshua Reynolds loved her but she was trapped into marriage by an impostor whom she had to pay off. In 1781 she married the Venetian **Antonio Zucchi** (1726-1795), who had travelled with Robert and James Adam through Italy, studying paintings and antiques and whom they had invited to London where he became an A.R.A. in 1770. After enjoying a huge success with their mythological compositions and idyllic classical landscapes with ruins, the Zucchis retired to Italy in 1783. Harewood was one of several great houses they helped Robert Adam to adorn.

Richard Buckle

Angelica Kaufmann seems to have stuck irregularly shaped pieces of paper together for her immaculately drawn antique scenes, whether in the ovals topping the mirrors in the Gallery (as above) or the roundels in the Music Room's ceiling.
Left: Biagio Rebecca. Overmantel in Old Library representing the Triumph of Homer.

The China Room

This perfect small room, which was called by Adam in his original design the Study, has also been a dressing room and a library and was converted in 1958 into a cabinet for the display of porcelain. The arched recesses in the east and south walls have been restored in accordance with Adam's drawings (now in the Soane Museum, London), with the difference that they hold china, not books.

Joseph Rose carried out the ceiling and the plaster roundels, one of which, at the south end of the east wall, is particularly engaging in its fantasy, depicting a female centaur suckling her young. The relief over the chimneypiece is based on a famous ancient Roman painting of the first century AD known as the Aldobrandini Marriage: a bridegroom is shown waiting expectantly while his bride is made ready by female attendants.

East cabinet

The Sèvres was collected in the early years of the nineteenth century by Edward, Viscount Lascelles (1764-1814), who died without succeeding his father. Although a part of the Lascelles collection was sold in 1965, this cabinet contains pieces of extreme beauty and rarity and more fine examples are displayed in other apartments.

The Royal porcelain factory of Sèvres, founded in 1753, produced some of the most perfect pieces of china that have ever been modelled, fired, and adorned with gilt or painting, and the best of these were made before 1789, when the Revolution brought lower aesthetic standards. Indeed after the death in 1764 of Mme. de Pompadour, whose inspired taste and steady patronage had animated the craftsmen of Sèvres, the imaginative richness of their porcelain began gradually to decrease.

The rare and luscious rose-pink Sèvres only came in in 1758 – and was not made after Mme. de Pompadour's death – but Harewood can boast three pieces dated 1757. Perhaps the most splendid of the pink pieces is the shell-shaped vase in the centre of the cabinet, painted by an unknown artist with a scene of two children with a fowling-net; this is imitated from an engraving by J.B. le Prince after Boucher. The two (fan-shaped) *vases hollandaise* with criss-cross pink and gold decoration may have been bought from the factory in 1758 by the Prince of Monaco. The apple-green pair with crossed ribbons are painted by Vieillard.

The splendid *bleu du roi* tea service (dated 1779) was a gift from the City of Paris to the unfortunate Queen Marie-Antoinette. Notice how the heavy gold foliage on the dark blue border of the tray sets off a fantastic painting of kingfisher delicacy, which shows a group of peasants watching the antics of a monkey and three dogs in human clothing. All the scenes painted on this tea service by Pierre-André le Guay seem to evoke some remembered day when itinerant mountebanks came from over the hills and half the inhabitants of this hamlet ran to watch the performing animals, leaving the summer landscape littered with musical instruments, and their houses guarded by children or dogs. On the teapot a child buys a print of Louis XVI from a pedlar and on one of the four saucers a Punch sleeps under a tree beside a silent drum.

South cabinet

Here are displayed part of two dinner services. The gold and white Crown Derby china belonged to the statesman George Canning, the present Lord Harewood's great-great-great-grandfather. The Stone Coquerel et le Gros service, made in Paris, is stamped within its green ivy borders with transferred views of celebrated monuments taken from engravings. The tureen and sauceboats have French scenes, such as Notre-Dame de Paris; the plates have British churches and country houses, such as Salisbury Cathedral, Glamis Castle, Holkham, Clumber and Harewood. This service was a gift of Queen Mary to Princess Mary.

Richard Buckle

A Stone Coquerel et le Gros plate with Clumber.

Bleu du roi Sèvres tray from the Marie-Antoinette tea service painted by le Guay, 1779.

A Crown Derby sauce boat from the Canning service.

Shell vase in rose Pompadour Sèvres porcelain painted with a scene after Boucher, 1757-60.

Princess Mary's Dressing Room

WHEN MY FATHER AND MOTHER CAME to live at Harewood in 1929 after my grandfather's death, Sir Herbert Baker (Lutyens's assistant on the grand project of New Delhi in India) was asked to design certain new features and supervise the restoration of others. This room was his largest new undertaking and, in the "Adam revival" scheme he devised, he incorporated various decorative features taken from the demolished Harewood House, Hanover Square. The fireplace recess with its two cupboards containing some of my mother's collection of amber, rose quartz and jade, has in the apse a nymph inspired by Botticelli and designed by *Sir Charles Wheeler, P.R.A.* To the left and right of it are the arms of Princess Mary and the sixth Earl of Harewood, the latter featuring Canning quarterings. The clock is by *Sarton* of Liège.

On the west wall is a pastel by *Francis Cotes* of Frances Lascelles, daughter of the 1st Earl of Harewood, and facing it the child's mother by the same artist.

Detail of clock by Sarton of Liège.

Left: Anne, daughter of William Chaloner of Guisborough, wife of the 1st Earl.

Three of the Coronation Chairs were used at the Coronation of King George VI in 1937, the fourth one at Queen Elizabeth II's in 1953. Whoever was invited to sit on them at the ceremony is by custom allowed to keep them.

17

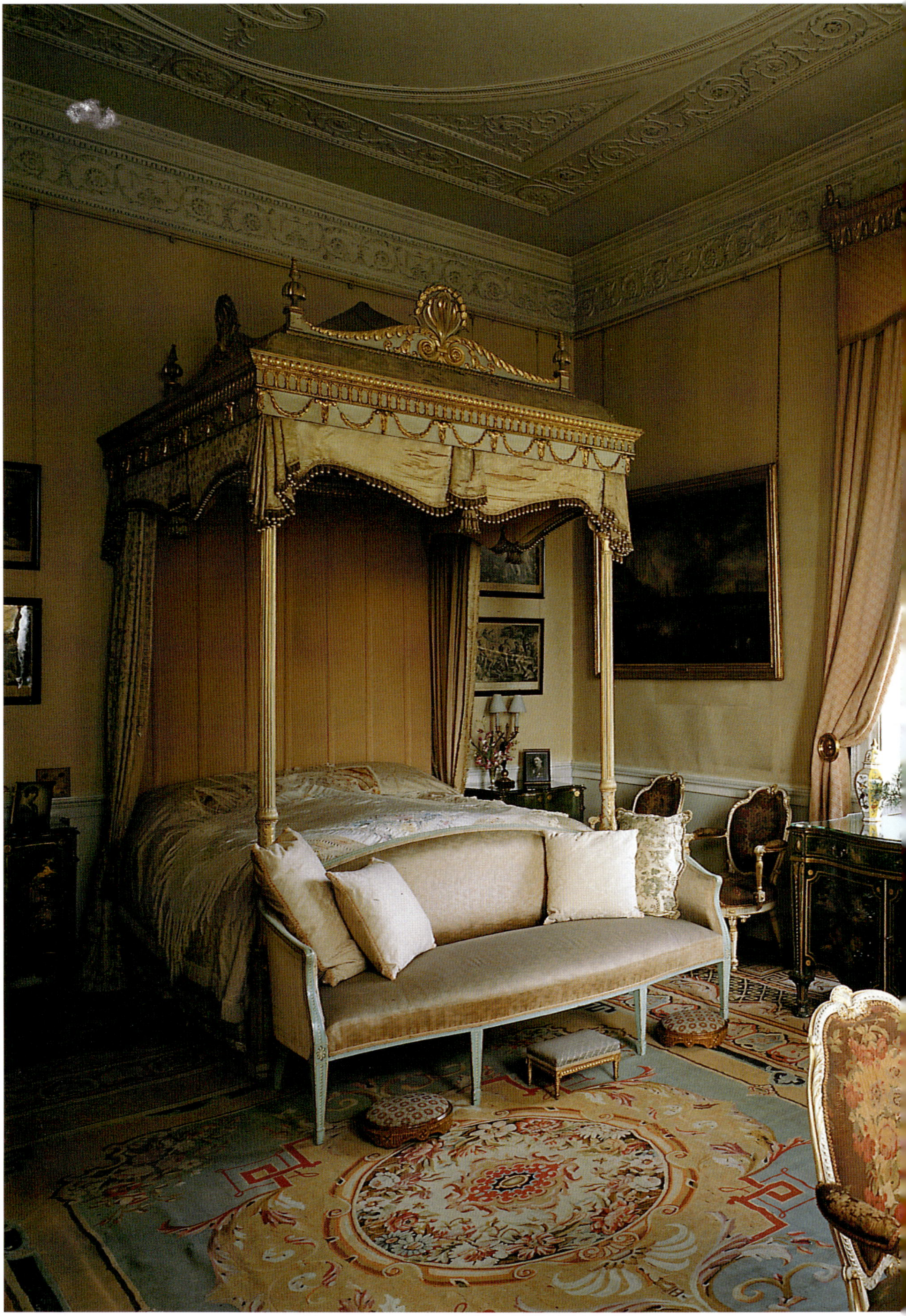

The East Bedroom

This was Edwin Lascelles's Bedroom, and his successors at Harewood seem to have followed his example in appropriating the room. Ceiling and frieze are designed by Adam, with a particularly seductive sunflower in the middle of the ceiling.

Pictures are a mixture of drawings of Italian scenes by non-Italian artists, of engravings, a Dutch seascape and an English landscape, whose subject – a view from Harewood up Wharfedale – has delighted generations of the Lascelles family and their friends.

Bed, chairs and lacquer furniture in the Chinese style are by Chippendale, the first big-scale encounter on this tour of the House with one of the artists who dominate its decorative schemes.

Chippendale clothes press.

Thomas Chippendale c.1718-1779

Thomas Chippendale's work can be seen throughout the House – chairs, sofas, beds, commodes, tables, mirrors, chests of drawers, console tables, sideboards, dining room furniture, library steps, picture frames, torchères, fire screens, pelmets, bookcases, clothes presses, bedside tables, stools, secretaires. No room is without an example of his work.

Chippendale did not confine himself to a single style. A taste for chinoiserie started to develop in England in mid-eighteenth century and Chippendale's efforts in this direction were often described by him, and even in the Harewood inventory after Edwin Lascelles's death, as Indian. In this room, the commode in the window, the two night tables and the clothes press between the windows – the lacquered surfaces decorated with oriental designs – are outstanding examples of this phase of Chippendale's art and craft.

Detail of bedside cabinet.

He fulfilled Edwin's commission from his workshop in St. Martin's Lane, London, and brought English furniture design and production to such new levels of sophistication and perfection that, perhaps for the first time, what was made in this country rivalled the more elaborate products of France.

The Watercolour Rooms

*Below: J.M.W. Turner, **Harewood House from the North East**. In this work which shows the house in the middle distance, Turner develops the human interest of his works, introducing some labourers resting after the effort of felling a tree.*

THE HAREWOOD COLLECTION OF watercolours is of national importance, containing early works by Turner, Girtin and Varley. Recent re-display at the house has now enabled us to devote two rooms exclusively to them. Due to the fragile nature of watercolours these rooms have been especially created with low light levels to protect the works and a system of rotation of works on an annual basis is in place so that different aspects of the collection can be displayed and re-interpreted.

Edward, Viscount Lascelles (1764 - 1814) was a great patron of the arts and commissioned works from J.M.W. Turner, Thomas Girtin, John Varley and John Sell Cotman. Edward was one of Turner's earliest patrons - the artist was only 22 years of age when he visited Harewood in 1797 and produced such superb works as **Harewood House from the North East** (see illustration), with its prominent inclusion of workers on the estate in the centre of the composition. The tree they have felled is being carried away in front of the house. Edward Lascelles also encouraged the career of Thomas Girtin, commissioning at least nineteen works from him, and he is said to have preferred Girtin over Turner. Another favourite was John Varley, of whose work Edward owned at least six examples, including charming views of the house: **Harewood House from the South** and **Harewood House from the North** painted on his 1803 visit to Yorkshire. These artists developed the technical and aesthetic weight of their watercolours to such an extent that they could rival the form and gravity of oil painting. The vogue in the early nineteenth century was to closely frame finished watercolours in gilt frames and display them as cabinet pictures on the wall. Many of the watercolours of this period which survive at Harewood have period frames and those which have not we have re-framed in sympathetic style so that when they are on display they give the impression of a contemporary connoisseur's cabinet in the early nineteenth century. Edward Lascelles actually displayed his works at the family home, Harewood House in Hanover Square, London. Unfortunately nearly all the watercolours in Edward Lascelles's original collection were sold at auction at Christie's on 1st May 1858, ostensibly because it was feared that they were fading. Fortunately more recent generations of the Lascelles family have been successful in re-acquiring watercolours, especially the 6th Earl and Princess Mary, who was particularly fond of watercolours.

The collection was also greatly expanded by the inheritance of the last Marquess of Clanricarde's works of art in 1916, which descended to the Lascelles family through marriage, and which included many fine nineteenth century watercolours. Most notable of these are the brightly coloured and detailed scenes of Greece and Italy by the Wakefield-born topographical artist *Thomas Hartley Cromek (1809-1873)*. In addition to this there are a large number of works by the Marquess's aunt, Charlotte, Countess Canning, a talented amateur watercolourist who was also lady-in-waiting to Queen Victoria. One work is actually by Queen Victoria herself dated 1848, a copy after Lady Canning. Other works in the collection include interesting eighteenth century local views such as *Moses Griffith's* **Brimham Rocks** and the **Harrogate Hot Wells.** These works were purchased by the 6th Earl of Harewood, as well as Malton's well-known view of the house. Every effort is made to regularly change the displays to enable this wide variety of works to be seen by the public while also preserving them for future generations.

Ann Sumner

Above: Thomas Girtin, **Harewood Bridge.** *A fascinating, almost monochromatic watercolour, acquired by Edward, Viscount Lascelles in 1801.*

Below: Thomas Hartley Cromek, **Arch of Titus, Rome,** *inherited by the 6th Earl of Harewood from the Marquess of Clanricarde.*

Lord Harewood's Sitting Room

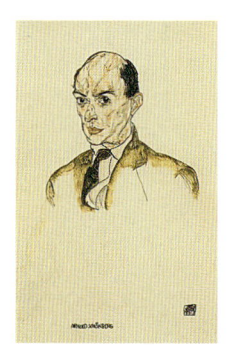

Top: **Mattia Battistini** *by Walter Sickert.*
Above: **Arnold Schoenberg** *by Egon Schiele.*

Above: **Nan Seated** *by Jacob Epstein.*
Above right: **Bolm and Karsavina** *by Henri Gaudier Brzeska.*

A CHEERFUL, UNPRETENTIOUS room whose views are, first, onto the East Garden and, to the South, over the Terrace, newly restored to Barry's design of the 1840s but still with a great bronze of **Orpheus** by *Astrid Zydower (born 1930)* in the middle. Capability Brown's landscape lies beyond.

The room is hung with pictures my wife and I have collected over the past thirty years, with no particular scheme in mind other than personal preference.

As you come in, you will see in front of you a striking picture by *Sir Sidney Nolan (1917-1992),* the great Australian painter, whose last exhibition, a retrospective, was held at Harewood and closed only a few weeks before he died. It is a late entry in the Ned Kelly series, for which he became famous in the years after the 1939-45 War. Another Nolan is in the centre of the wall on your right, a Chinese landscape painted in the 1980s on one of the artist's many foreign expeditions. On the wall on your left, the East side of the room, hang three small pictures by *Walter Sickert (1860-1942),* part of his so-called Camden Town Murder series, inspired by a lurid murder in the part of London where the painter lived.

On the right-hand side of the window, a lithograph with a lively football subject by *Pablo Picasso (1881-1973),* and **Dravidian Heads** by *M.F. Husain (born 1915),* a leading Indian painter. On the South wall between the windows and the Nolan, a portrait of the composer **Arnold Schoenberg** by the great and once controversial Viennese artist *Egon Schiele (1890-1918),* and above it a drawing of a Greek boy by *John Craxton (born 1922).* Also on the South wall, the other side of the window, **Skate and Unicorn** by *Arthur Boyd (born 1920),* another leading contemporary Australian painter and Sidney Nolan's brother-in-law. Underneath Nolan's Chinese view hang three little gouaches of Harewood by *John Piper (1903-1992).* On the North wall, to the right of the fireplace you will find **Wrestlers** *(1937)* by the French naïve painter *Camille Bombois (1883-1970)* and, over the door, **Landscape in the Languedoc** by the Frenchman *Jean Hugo (1894-1984).* Above the bookcase on the left, another picture by *M.F. Husain* of a traditional Indian subject: the lascivious god Krishna climbs a tree in order to watch a group of naked Gopis at their ablutions. Above the door as you leave, Sickert's impression of the great singer **Mattia Battistini** in action during his farewell tour of this country. Battistini was at one time known as 'La Gloria d'Italia' – the glory of Italy. Two drawings of my wife and myself made by *David Hankinson* in 1987 hang by the door.

Bronzes in this room are by *Henri Gaudier Brzeska (1891-1915):* the Russian dancers **Bolm and Karsavina** in Stravinsky's ballet "The Firebird"; *Sir Jacob Epstein (1880-1959):* **Nan Seated** *(1911);* and *Austin Bennett:* heads of my wife and myself.

From this room, for the first time for 150 years or more, the *enfilade* provided for and presumably envisaged by Carr, Adam and Edwin Lascelles can be seen and enjoyed; or, in simpler terms, you can see from one end of the House to the other without interruption – a feature, sometimes obscured by later meddling hands, of many old houses.

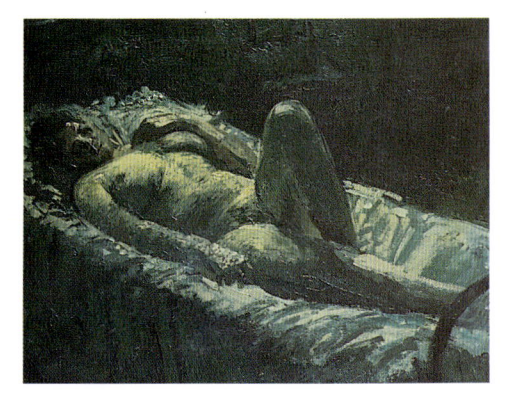

Left and above: two paintings from Walter Sickert's 'Camden Town Murder' series.

THE ANTE ROOM next door is dominated by three equestrian pictures by *Sir Alfred Munnings (1878-1959)*, one of my mother riding in the summer ("my best equestrian open-air portrait", said the artist), two more concerned with the Bramham Moor hunt, one with Almscliff in the distance. Also, two charcoal drawings of my mother and father by *John Singer Sargent (1856-1925);* two others of my grandparents by the court painter *Frank Salisbury (1874-1962)* and a further Salisbury of my mother, this time a sketch in oils. On the North wall, Lord Clanricarde (who left my father his estate), and on the East, my aunt Lady Boyne and one of my father in First World War uniform. Next to the door by which you entered, a small portrait of my brother, the Hon. Gerald Lascelles, aged three, and over the door by which you leave, Sargent's painting of the Grand Council Chamber in the Doge's Palace in Venice.

Right: Trompe l'oeil bookcase in the Ante Room.

23

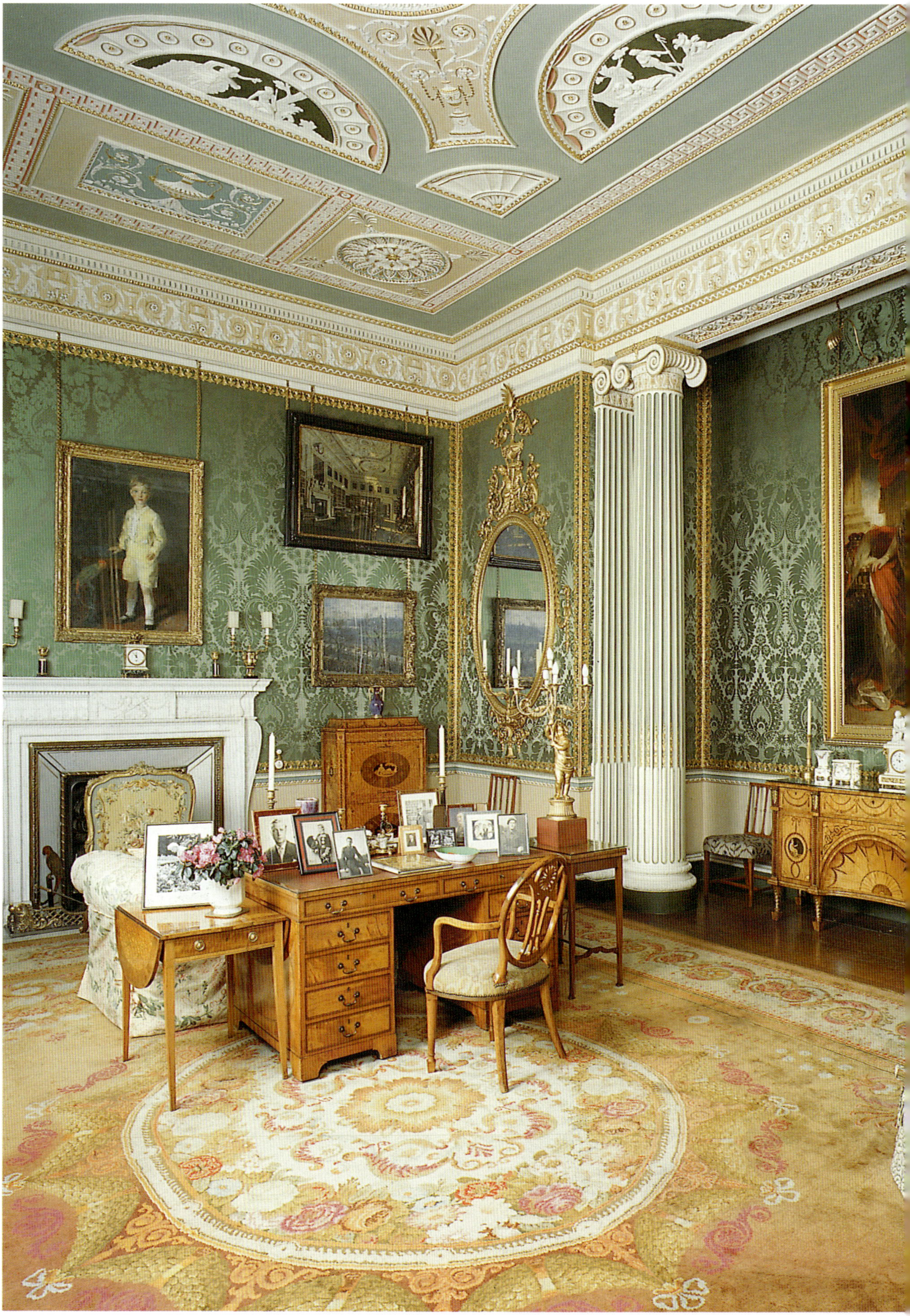

Princess Mary's Sitting Room

THIS ROOM WAS DESIGNED AS THE STATE Bedroom, reserved apparently for visiting royalty but transformed by Barry in the 1840s to a sitting room. The ceiling colours are now, after a paint scrape, known to be those chosen by Robert Adam. The green silk on the walls has been woven in France, an exact copy of the original pattern. The splendid Chippendale mirrors, made for this room in the early 1770s, have until recently been in storage at Harewood *(see panel on page 31).*

Portraits include, over the chimney piece, the only one in oils of me in this house, by *Ambrose McEvoy (1878-1927),* painted when I was four (the wooden parrot stands near the picture); and elsewhere of the **Prince Consort** by *Franz Xavier Winterhalter (1805-1873),* of my father by *Solomon J. Solomon (1860-1927),* of my mother as a girl by *Mrs Adrian Hope,* and of Queen Mary by *Frank Salisbury (1874-1962).* The two large paintings are – in the recess – of **Jane Lady Harewood,** Edwin's wife, by *Henry Singleton (1766-1839);* and to the right, of **Mrs Scott and her daughter Henrietta,** afterwards Duchess of Portland, by *Richard Cosway (1742-1821).*

Also to be seen are the wedding procession of my parents by *Sir John Lavery (1874-1941),* the library of Chesterfield House, my parents' first London home by

Mrs Scott and her daughter by Richard Cosway.

Richard Jack (1866-1952); and Salisbury's painting of my mother signing the register at Westminster Abbey, February 28th 1922, watched by my four grandparents.

In addition to the splendid mirrors, Chippendale is responsible for three outstanding pieces of furniture in the room, a secretaire and two commodes, the largest (in the recess), with its ivory inlay and nobility of line, is often referred to as his finest creation.

Chippendale commode. One of his finest pieces of furniture, probably his most famous.

The Spanish Library

Originally the State Dressing Room *en suite* with the State Bedroom, this room was transformed by Barry into a Victorian library. Between the tall bookcases and the ceiling is a 17th century wall-covering of Spanish leather put there by my father to hide the heavy paint with which Barry covered both the small wall space in this room and the considerable amount in the Library next door. Busts of various periods connect bookcases and ceiling and on the chimneypiece are two exquisite cranes in porcelain of the reign of Ch'ien Lung.

On the table stands a bronze head of the young Queen Victoria, who as a girl of fifteen, stayed in this room when she visited Harewood; near it is a photograph at the time of her Diamond Jubilee in 1897, sixty-two years later. Elsewhere, photographs of the next five sovereigns of this country, either grouped on the Royal Yacht Britannia, or on the occasion of the Coronations of 1937 and 1953. The King's command to my grandfather to attend the Coronation of 1902 and a white bust of Princess Alexandra of Denmark at the time of her engagement to the English Prince of Wales stand in the middle of the table. To the left, Queen Marie of Romania. On the table to the right, my parents' wedding group. To the left are my mother's four brothers, *(l to r)* the Duke of Kent, the Prince of Wales, the Duke of York (later King George VI) and the Duke of Gloucester.

Family photographs and memorabilia. The framed print shows King Edward VII with his son and grandson, the future Kings George V and Edward VIII, on the Royal Yacht Britannia.

Chippendale's oblong library steps open out to a practical height and are ornamented with marquetry on a rosewood ground.

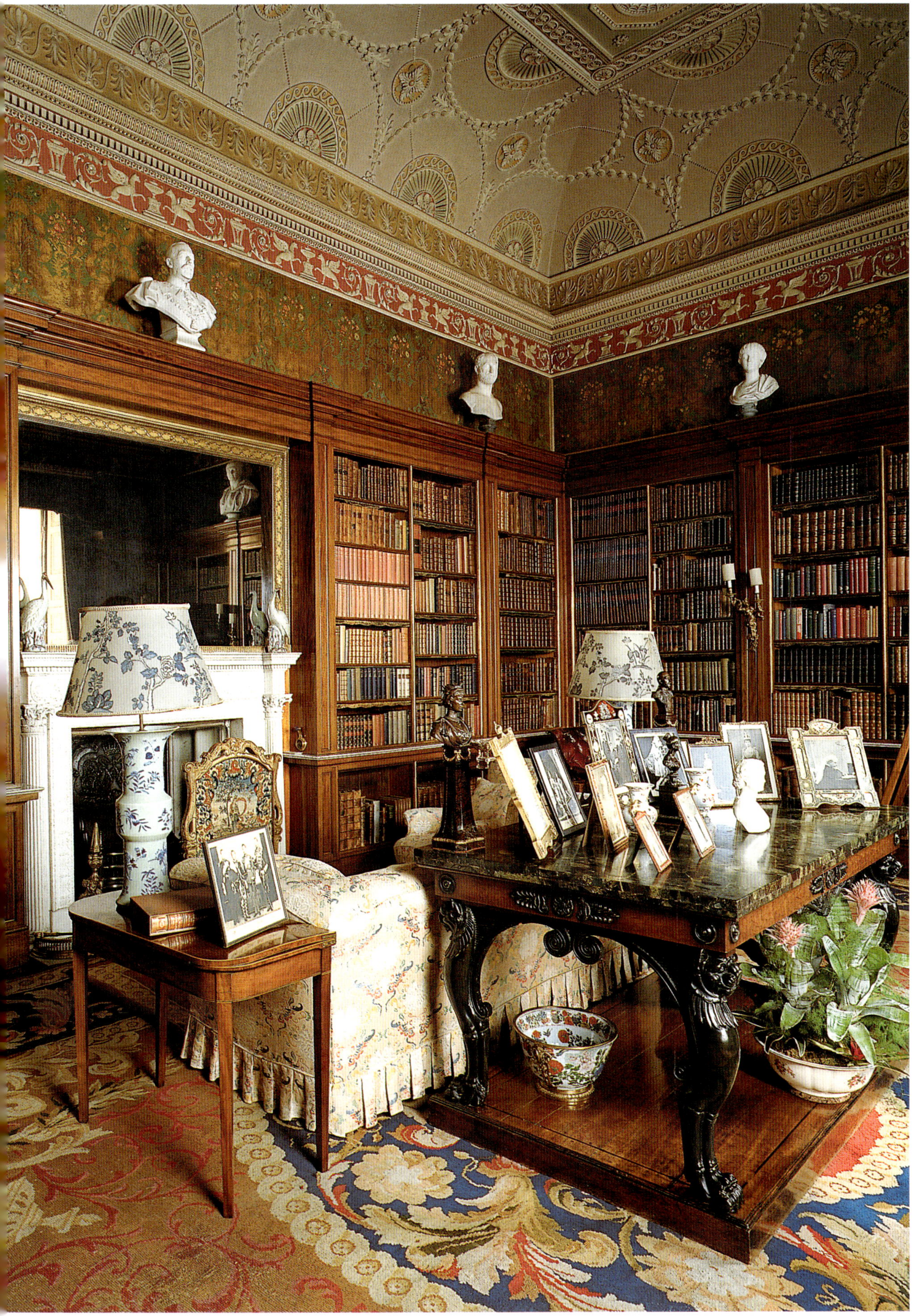

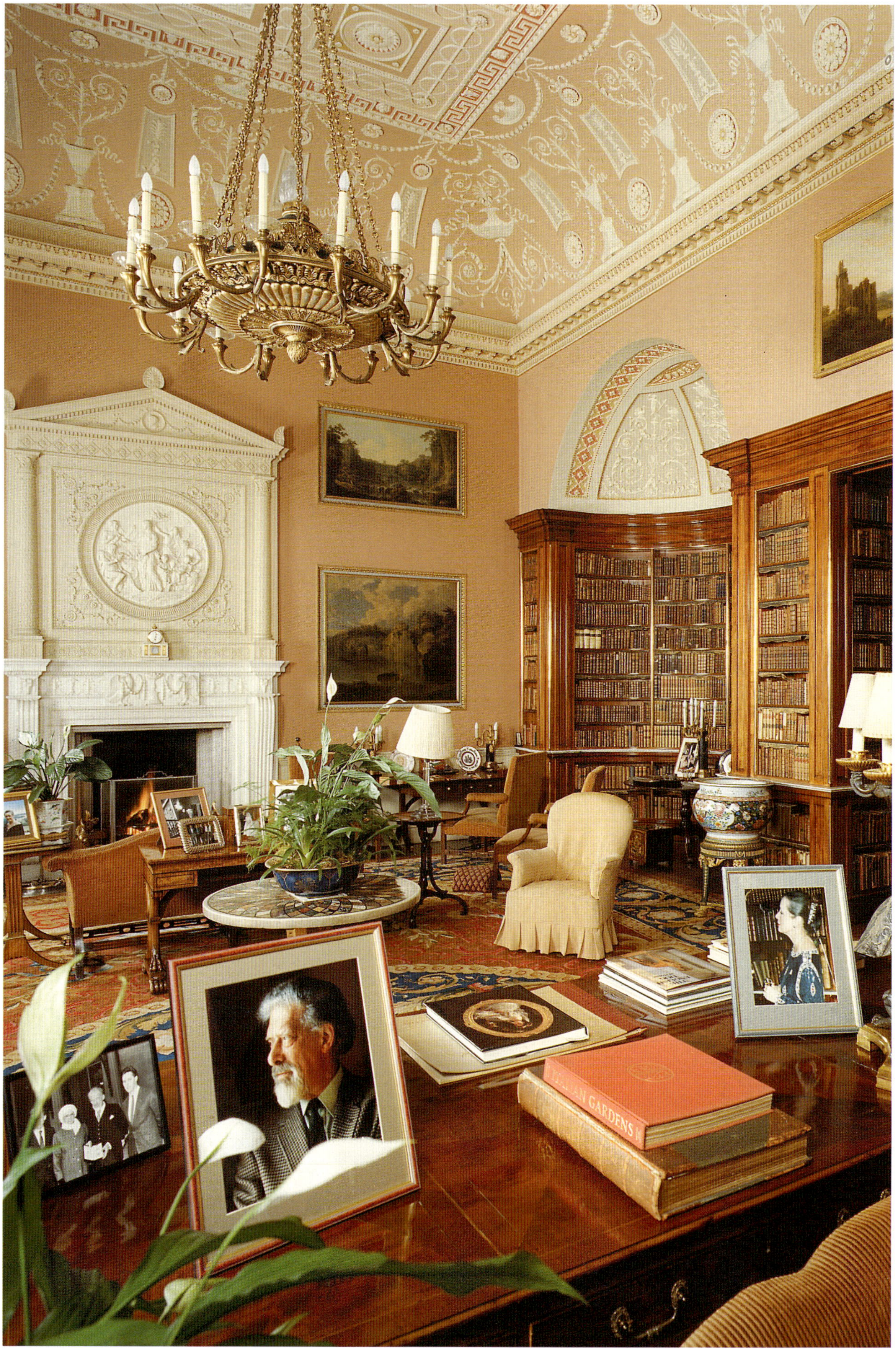

The Library

The Library, known in the past as the Saloon, is a mainly Victorian room dominated by Barry's imposing mahogany bookcases with their brass inlay and marble chair rail. It maintains stylistic contact with an earlier century through Adam's spectacular ceiling together with his chimneypieces and plaster overmantels with their round, sculptured reliefs by *Collins*. "Some Adam ceilings are rectilinear and heroic, such as that in the Entrance Hall, others are delicate, such as that in the East Bedroom; this one might be described as 'symphonic', with its motifs and colours which ebb, flow, swell, repeat themselves and dissemble into one tremendous scheme", says Richard Buckle with some justification in an earlier guide book.

When I first knew the room, the ceiling was green with elements of blue, red and gold, and the walls were covered in dark blue and chocolate paint with a regular gold pattern (as too the Spanish Library). Bookcases and paint together produced a note of unintended gloom, and there was little reconciliation between walls and ceiling. The choice of terracotta as a colour basis was made in 1958 in an attempt to accommodate Barry's monumentality and Adam's fantasy in a room which since Barry's transformation has been the central living room of the House.

There are four objects supplied by the Royal Clockmaker, *Benjamin Vulliamy*. The ormolu-mounted marble-cased clock (on the chimneypiece) is signed and was made about 1796; the bronze tazza on the table in the right-hand alcove was supplied in 1804; and the black, marble and ormolu-mounted lamps are signed "Vulliamy London AD 1811".

Pictures

Originally, all four decorative landscapes by *Nicholas Dall* (a Dane, who died in London in 1777) were over doors (four local views – **Harewood Castle, Aysgarth Force, Knaresborough, Richmond**). High over the north door hangs another picture of Harewood Castle by *Michael Rooker (1743-1801)*.

In the last years of the 18th century and long before Barry's alteration of 1844-5, Harewood's new owner must already have had ideas of turning the room from a central concourse into something more habitable. Two doors were suppressed and replaced by pictures of Plompton Rocks by *J.M.W. Turner*, his earliest oil paintings *(1798)* and the only oils by him in the House.

Ormolu-mounted marble-cased clock by Benjamin Vulliamy.

*Above: **Plompton Rocks** by J.M.W. Turner, painted in 1798 and one of the two oils by him at Harewood.*

Left: Adam's elaborate and beautiful overmantel with Collins's sculptured relief. Collins worked in plaster but at least by 1819 the roundels were painted and the earliest guide book describes them as bronze! Marble is the state towards which they now aspire.

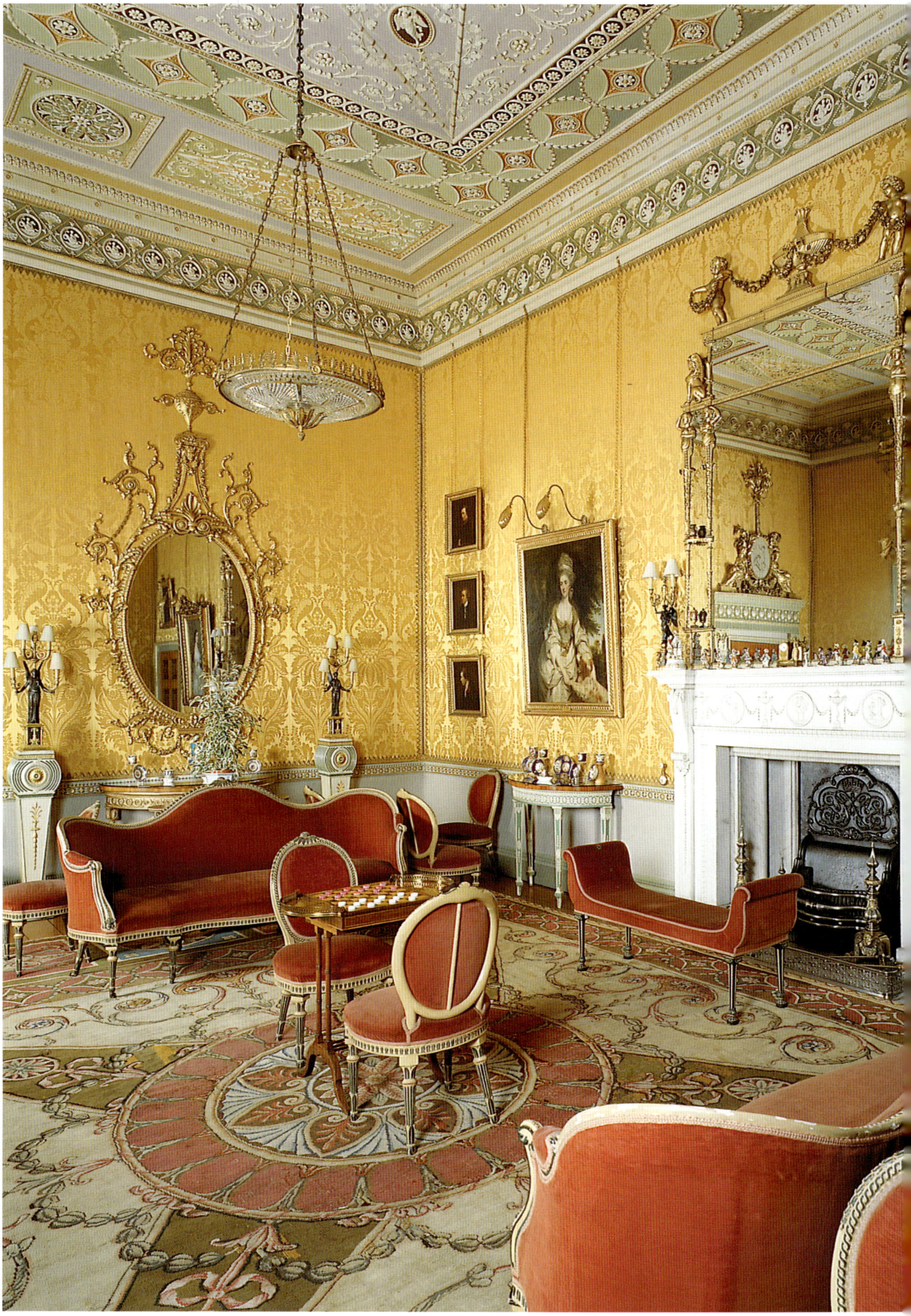

The Yellow Drawing Room

Consistency of motif was something Adam regularly sought and in this room the star and circle of the carpet echo without slavishly copying the ceiling; the lozenges in the frieze running round the cornice contain plaques with cupids riding sea-horses and this is repeated over the doors; all the chairs and sofas luxuriate in the sunflower open on their backs. In the nineteenth and early twentieth centuries, the room was used as a Billiard Room, but it was originally known as the Yellow Drawing Room – Edwin Lascelles, after work on decorating the House had begun, bought yellow silk for the walls and Adam was obliged to re-vamp his colour scheme for the ceiling. A day book for September 1769 mentions painting "a specimen of colours for Mr. Adam's approbation" and a recent paint scrape confirmed the colours now on the ceiling, restored like the silk-bedecked walls to fit eighteenth century ideas.

Two great looking glasses by Chippendale dominate the room, like others in the House partly stripped of their ornamentation by the Victorians and in 1993-4 painstakingly restored by Carvers and Gilders.

Adelina Patti (1843-1919), by Winterhalter.

Competition with them is provided by two female portraits, **Mrs. Hardinge** (a family connection) by *Sir Joshua Reynolds (1723-1792)* to the left of the chimneypiece, and to the right, the highly decorative portrait of **Adelina Patti**, the great 19th century opera singer by *Winterhalter*.

Chippendale Mirrors

In 1844-5, **Sir Charles Barry** remodelled the principal storey of the House, drastically altering several rooms and sweeping others away entirely, including the so-called Circular Dressing Room (which much later became the Lift Room).

During these alterations, a number of furnishings (including mirrors with elaborate peripheral ornaments) were dismantled and removed to store where they remained untouched until the mid-1980s. Christopher Gilbert, in his invaluable *Life and Work of Thomas Chippendale* (1978), illustrates some of these pieces as they were before the recent extensive programme of sorting and repair was undertaken at the instigation of Hugh Roberts (then at Christie's, now Deputy Surveyor of the Queen's Works of Art) and through the expertise and craftsmanship of Carvers and Gilders.

31

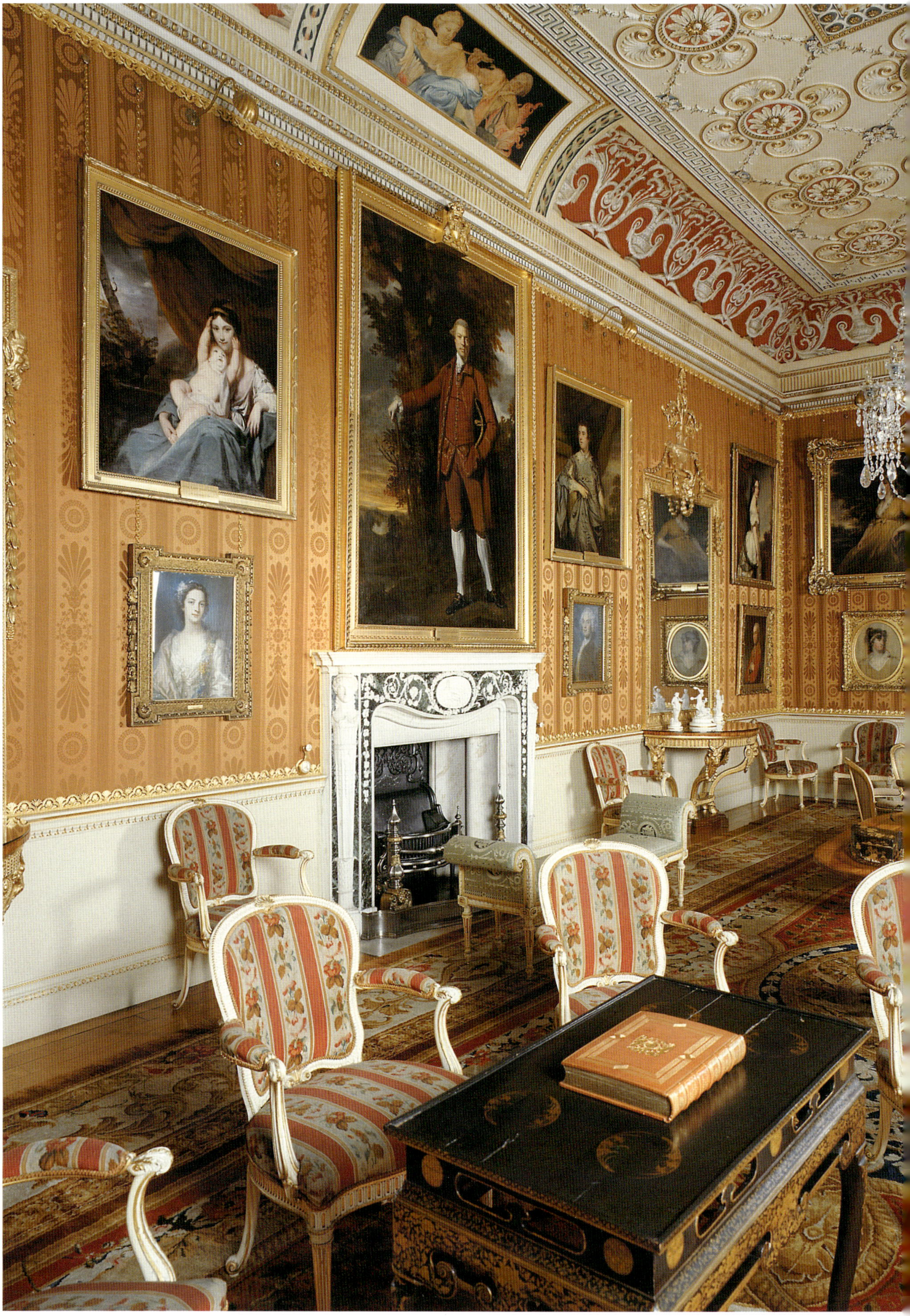

The Cinnamon Drawing Room

ORIGINALLY, AS THE early guide book tells us, hung with white damask and bordered with gold, the room was known as the White Drawing Room and featured no fewer than five looking glasses as well as two full length family portraits. The white silk was later replaced by green which gradually faded until the recent decision to concentrate family portraits of a certain period in this room prompted the present cinnamon background.

The furniture is by *Chippendale* and at either end are particularly fine gilt tables on the subject of whose tops Percy Macquoid in his book on English furniture was nothing short of lyrical: "the blues, greens, purples and deep amber gold of the delicately drawn inlay possesses the lustre and colour of a peacock's back". They were made for the Music Room but transferred to allow visitors easier access.

The **Rams head pier glasses** were originally in the Dining Room (now redesigned and enlarged by Barry to a scale which will no longer accommodate them) and they were, in 1989, reunited with the console tables which properly belong underneath them so that they now stand together for the first time for nearly 150 years. Victorian taste had decided to remove the elaborate urns and ornaments which proliferate above the frames as well as the festoons which hang from the satyrs on either side. All this filigree was found in a store room of the Joiners' Shop in the Estate Yard, neatly packed away and labelled, and the mirrors have been painstakingly rebuilt over two years, the first of several pairs to undergo this treatment before being restored to places of honour in the house.

Alfred Stevens was invited in 1852, newly returned from Italian studies, to supply additional paintings for the cove and centre of Adam's ceiling, a piece of *lèse-majesté* excused maybe by the brilliance with which he executed his commission.

The **China figures** on the table are modern Biscuit de Sèvres, given to my parents as a wedding present by the City of Paris.

Biscuit de Sèvres figures.

Chippendale pier table.

Above: **Lady Worsley** *by Sir Joshua Reynolds.*

Right: **Lady Louisa Lascelles** *by Sir Thomas Lawrence.*

Far right: **Henrietta, Lady Harewood** *by John Hoppner.*

PICTURES

Most English country houses have interesting family portraits and those seen here are representative of the best portrait painters of the 18th and early 19th centuries.

Six are by *Sir Joshua Reynolds P.R.A. (1723-1792).* Over the chimneypiece, **Edwin Lascelles,** who built the house and in his plum-coloured suit surveys his relatives as the sun, rather improbably, sets almost due north of his new house. At either end of the room over Chippendale's gilt pier tables are Edwin's two step-daughters, **Lady Harrington,** demurely humorous (next to the door by which you enter), and her sister **Lady Worsley,** dashing in her red riding dress and notorious for her amorous escapades. On either side of the fireplace can be seen **Edward, 1st Earl of Harewood** in Van Dyck fancy dress, aged 22, and his wife **Anne,** with her infant daughter, Frances (Reynolds's portrait of her sister Mrs Hale is in the Music Room). Next to the mirror to the left of the fireplace, the lower of two pictures, **Henry, 2nd Earl of Harewood.**

On either side of the fireplace are two smaller pastel portraits by *George Knapton (1698-1778)* of **Edwin Lascelles** and his first wife, **Elizabeth,** daughter and heir of Sir Darcy Dawes.

Next to Lady Worsley hangs **George Canning** as a boy by *Thomas Gainsborough (1727-1788),* probably painted as Canning

*Far left: **Edward, 1st Earl of Harewood** by Reynolds.*

*Left: **13th Earl of Clanricarde** by Romney.*

left Eton and therefore one of Gainsborough's last works. Canning was my great-great-great-grandfather, as was **John, Earl of Clanricarde,** whose portrait in red military uniform by *George Romney (1734-1802)* hangs low on the extreme right of the North wall (their granddaughter married the 4th Lord Harewood).

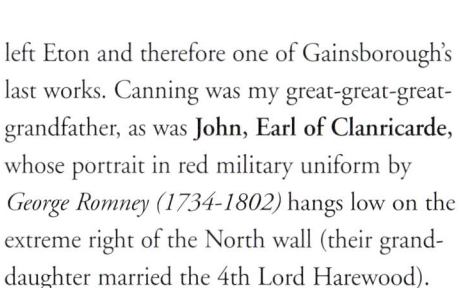

Prominent in the room are three portraits by *John Hoppner (1758-1810):* on the West wall (next to Lady Worsley and above George Canning), **Henrietta, Countess of Harewood,** herself a proficient draughtswoman and painted young and at ease in a lilac-coloured dress; opposite her, on the East wall, her sister-in-law, **Lady Mary York,** round and comfortable in yellow silk; and, over the door by which you leave the room, **Edward, Viscount Lascelles,** who died before he succeeded his father, was plump and charming, the friend of Turner, Girtin and Hoppner and collector of the china in the house. He was thought in his time to resemble the Prince Regent, who resented the idea and referred to him as "The Pretender".

Four pictures remain. *Sir Thomas Lawrence (1769-1830):* an unfinished portrait of **Lady Louisa Lascelles,** daughter of the 2nd Earl of Harewood (underneath Lady Mary York); another portrait of **Henrietta** by *John Jackson (1778-1831),* over the door by which you came in; at the far end of the North wall,

a portrait by an unidentified English artist *c.*1730 of **Edward Lascelles,** who died in Barbados in 1747 and was father of the man Reynolds painted in fancy dress; finally, **Harriet Canning,** the Prime Minister's daughter, by *Richard Buckner (flourished 1842-1877),* on extreme right of the North wall (she became Lady Clanricarde and was my great-great-grandmother).

*Above: **George Canning** by Gainsborough.*

*Left: **Lady Harrington** by Reynolds.*

The Gallery

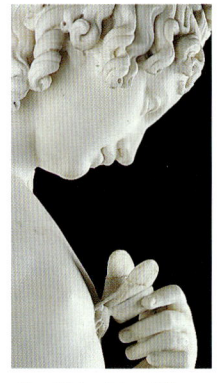

Cupid by John Gibson.

"This room extends over the whole west end of the house, and is 76 feet 10 inches by 24 feet 3 inches, 21 feet 3 inches high; it is truly elegant, and presents such a show of magnificence and art as eye hath seldom seen and words cannot describe" – so some 50 years after it was built wrote John Jewell in the earliest guide book to Harewood, before proceeding to deny its final proposition. It was one of Adam's most magnificent achievements, but not immune on that account to alterations under Barry's aegis. Columns supporting the central arches of the three triple windows, at either end and in the middle, were replaced by brackets (a favourite device of Barry's, it would appear); and the chimneypiece, for which Adam's design is dated 1776, was removed to the Dining Room and two Victorian replacements installed. We have now restored the chimneypiece to its original position and placed the later pair (which, however handsome, were unquestionably intruders on Adam's scheme) in store, and the main windows are again graced by the pillars and pilasters which, says Jewell's guide book, were "painted by Mr. Hutchinson, of London, in imitation of the verd antique marble and admirably transcribed from a table in the same room".

John Jewell describes the ceiling as of the palmyran taste; Adam drew it in 1769 and Rose executed it within a couple of years, its "oblongs, crosses, ovals and octagons, adorned with urns, bows, masks, festoons, rosettes, acanthus, daisy and honeysuckle" (the description is Richard Buckle's). The exploits, amorous, war-like, or simply ceremonial, of Greek gods and goddesses are depicted on the

Chinese vase with Vulliamy decoration.

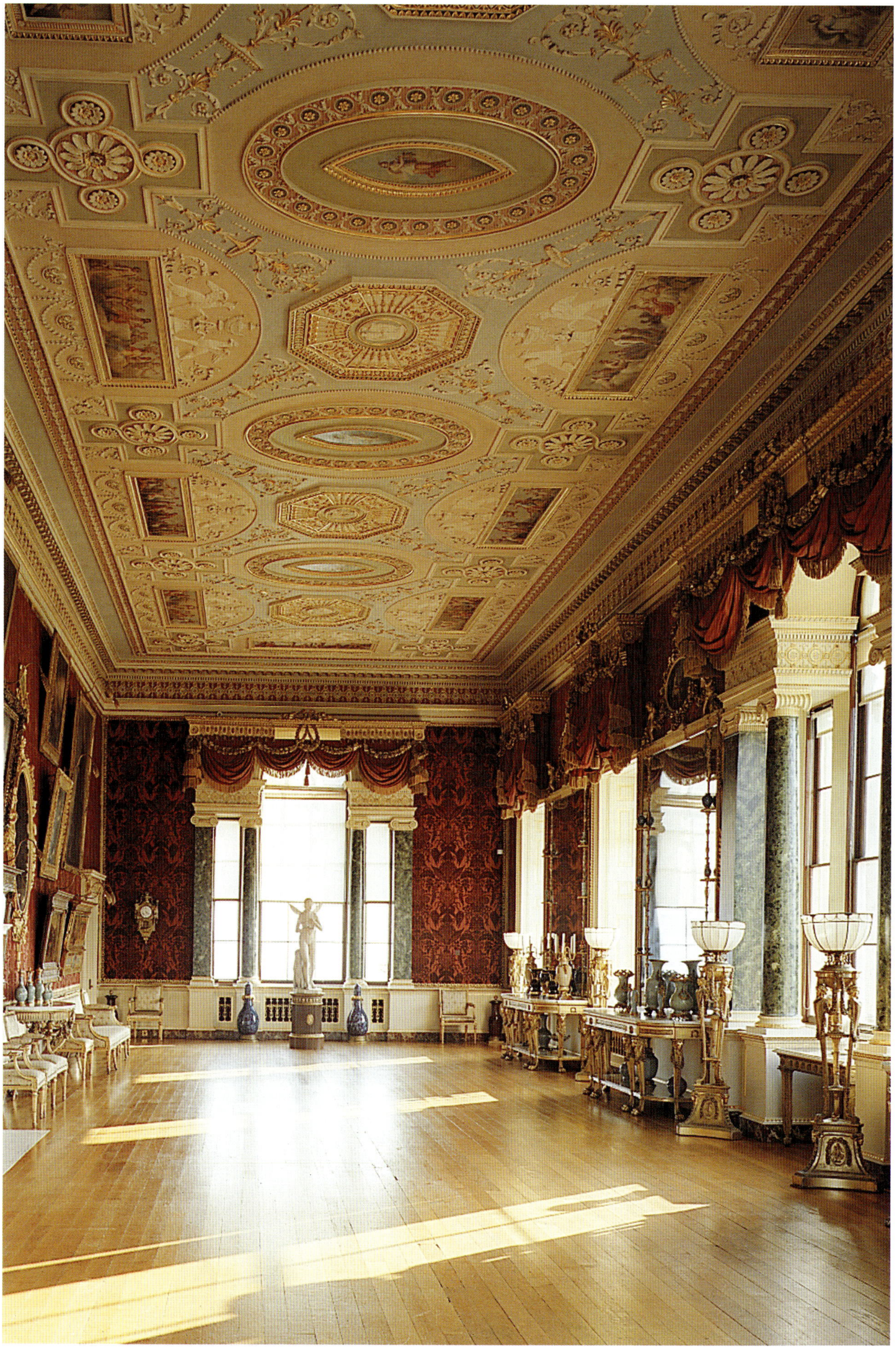

ceiling by *Biagio Rebecca* (see page 15), and four decorative oval paintings by *Angelica Kaufmann* (see page 15) top the mirrors between the windows. These, with their elegantly flanking cherubs, stand to the credit of *Thomas Chippendale,* as do the rectilinear chairs and sofas, and the elegant torchères (candelabra stands to which were added in the 1930s inverted shades for casting light on the ceiling). To crown Chippendale's achievement here – a celebrated feature of the room – are the **pelmets,** beautifully carved to imitate a heavy material – the only 'curtains' the room was intended to have. The marble-topped console tables with their rams' heads and lions' feet on which the mirrors rest are later and by the younger Chippendale.

The Chippendale mirrors on the East wall were, according to Christopher Gilbert, probably designed for the Gallery but (on the evidence of the watercolour of that date by Scarlett Davis) displaced by the 1820s. Some decorative elements, removed perhaps to reduce height so as to accommodate the mirrors in another and lower room, have recently been restored.

Elsewhere may be found *Thorwaldsen's* head of an Italian girl (early 19th century), and early 19th century marble figures of **Psyche** by *Lorenzo Bartolini* and **Cupid** by *John Gibson.*

CHINA

Richard Buckle writes: "The Gallery houses the famous Harewood collection of **Chinese Porcelain.** It is instructive to consider the history of these fragile works of art. By the time of the Ming Emperors the various refinements of turning, carving, engraving, painting in underglaze, crackling, firing, enamelling and gilding had been perfected at the factory of Ching-Tê-Chên, near Peking. These vases and bowls, either in plain colours – celadon green, *clair de lune* (pale moon-light-blue), *sang de boeuf* (bull's blood) or lavender – or enamelled with cocks, peacocks, peonies or plum-blossom in the styles known as *famille verte* and *famille rose,* were mostly executed during the reigns of the emperors K'ang Hsi, Yung Cheng and Ch'ien Lung, that is to say between 1662 and 1795. Exported to France, they were used almost as a base on which French craftsmen in ormolu (gilded bronze) could demonstrate their invention and skill; they were given richly-chased rims, pedestals and handles in styles ranging from the florid rococo of the mid-18th century to the severe and rigid neo-classicism of the Empire. As their aristocratic collectors fell victim to the Revolution, so these treasures appeared in the Paris salerooms; and in 1802, when so many English people took advantage of the Peace of Amiens to dash over to Paris, the collection was begun by Edward Lascelles, son of the 1st Earl, who brought it to Harewood House, Hanover Square, and eventually to Yorkshire.

In addition to those decorated in France, three blue Chinese vases were mounted with ormolu ornaments for Edward Lascelles in 1806 by Vulliamy. They stand on the left hand console table".

Above: A watercolour by John Scarlett Davis, probably painted in 1827 and showing the gallery in almost its current manifestation.

Left: Chippendale's beautifully carved pelmets.

Below: Clair de Lune K'ang Hsi fish vase in Louis XV ormolu mount.

Top left: Bellini: Madonna and Child with Donor.

Top right: Titian: Francis I.

Above: Cima: St. Jerome in the desert.

PICTURES

When the house was first built, there seem to have been few if any pictures in this room, where Edwin Lascelles must have relied on the decorative skills of Adam and Chippendale to make an effect, but by the 1820s it had become the focus for family portraits. In 1989-90, it was decided not only to re-decorate the room, which had become shabby with age and as a result of floods from the floor above it (to say nothing of a fire at the end of the last century), but, on the advice of Alec Cobbe*, to concentrate in the Gallery the Italian pictures collected in the decade after the 1914-18 War by my father. Some were sold to pay death duties but what remain, slightly augmented to allow for an Italianate hanging scheme, are to be found here.

East wall (from right to left and top to bottom: only pictures with lights are described.)

Alessandro Longhi (Venetian, 1733-1813). **The Procurator Mocenigo.** Alessandro was the son of the celebrated Pietro and the Mocenigos were one of the leading families of Venice, providing no fewer than seven Doges.

Appollonio di Giovanni (worked in Florence between 1445 and 1465). Two fronts of *cassoni* or marriage chests (the pendant is in a corresponding place on the far side of the Gallery). The subject is the **Rape of the Sabines.** On the right, Romulus entertains the Sabines to a feast at which the Romans provide acrobatic displays. His raised right hand is the signal for attack and in the centre of the panel the Romans set upon their unsuspecting guests. The other panel shows the **Generosity of Scipio**, who after capturing Carthage, united a beautiful young girl with her betrothed (left of the panel) and presided over her wedding feast (right).

Annibale Caracci (Bolognese, 1560-1609). **Portrait of a Gentleman** (or possibly the Artist as a gardener).

Giovanni Battista Cima da Conegliano (Venetian, c.1460-1518). **St. Jerome in the desert.** The penitent St. Jerome kneels before his crucifix, his lion on guard in a dried-up, golden landscape, beyond which can be seen a hill town, mountains and the sea. A falcon, two partridges, a kingfisher, a snake and a lizard are witnesses of the ecstasy of this cardinal-hermit who translated the Vulgate.

Titian, really Tiziano Vecellio (Venetian, 1485-1576). **Francis I.** Titian probably painted the distinctive profile of the French King from a medal, and the picture is a study for the portrait now in the Louvre. Francis I built the Château de Chambord, was the patron of Leonardo da Vinci as well as Titian and was the original of the amorous monarch in Victor Hugo's play 'Le Roi s'amuse' and Verdi's opera 'Rigoletto'.

Giovanni Bellini (Venetian, 1430/40-1516). **Madonna and Child with Donor.** One of two versions of Madonna and Child at Harewood by the painter who perhaps more than any other established the subject as paramount among religious themes. This wonderful picture was already in England in 1840, and in it Bellini demonstrates a closer approach to naturalism than in the Madonna and Child the other side of the fireplace, as demonstrated by the rings of tiredness around the eyes of the mother.

Veronese, really Paolo Caliari (Venetian, c.1528-1588). **Portrait of a Gentleman.** When exhibited in 1988-9 in Washington, this splendid portrait, a subtle pattern of blacks and whites, was assigned to Veronese's last years and described as 'A Gentleman of the Soranzo Family'.

El Greco, really Doménico Theotocópoulos (born Crete c. 1541, died Toledo 1614). **Allegory.** The meaning remains obscure. The picture is one of three still in existence on the same subject: the earliest, perhaps painted in Rome *c.*1570-5, now in the Prado, this picture, painted soon after El Greco's arrival

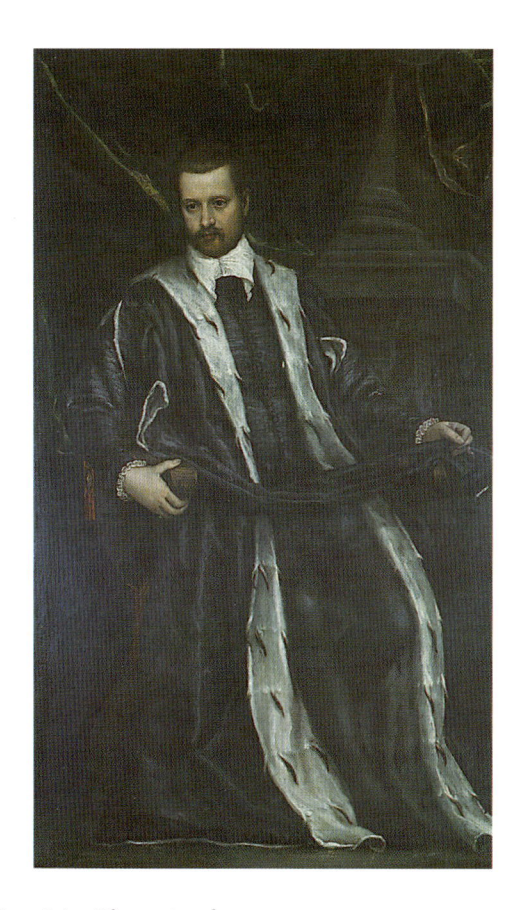

Veronese: **Portrait of a Gentleman.**

*Picture restorer and deviser of decorative schemes at Harewood and elsewhere.

Left: El Greco: **Allegory.**

Right: Tintoretto: An Admiral.

Below left: Sodoma: St. Jerome.

Below right: Lotto: Portrait of an old man.

in Toledo 1577-8; and a later example, also painted in Toledo c.1585, now in Edinburgh. The central figure was once thought to be female, but its close resemblance to the marvellous 'Boy lighting a candle' at the Capodimonte Museum in Naples demands a different interpretation.

The catalogue of an exhibition at the National Gallery of Scotland in 1989 suggests a relationship to the proverb 'A whore will set a candle to the devil', pointing also to the curiosity evinced by the monkey (chained in this version and therefore perhaps a symbol of man enslaved by the devil, or by sexual passion), matched by the curiosity of the man grinning foolishly on the right. At all events, and even if it was El Greco himself who devised the subject, the picture has overtones of the diabolical.

Tintoretto, really *Jacopo Robusti (Venetian, 1518-1594).* **An Admiral, perhaps Benedetto Soranzo.** At the naval battle of Lepanto in 1571, with his men dead and the Turks aboard his ship, Soranzo set fire to the magazine and blew up ship, enemy and himself.

Giovanni Bellini. **Madonna and Child.**

Lorenzo Lotto (Venetian, 1480-1556). **Portrait of an old man.** Roger Fry in 1920 refers to "the thin painting, with its almost exaggerated nervousness" and says it was painted at a late stage of Lotto's career.

Vincenzo Catena (Venetian, 1480-1531). **Madonna and Child with St. John the Baptist and St. Jerome.** When the picture was in the collection of William Beckford, builder of the ill-fated Fonthill Abbey, it was attributed to Bellini, Catena's teacher, and it has something of that master's serenity.

Giovanni Bazzi, called *Il Sodoma (Sienese, 1477-1549).* **St. Jerome.** The painting was once attributed to Leonardo da Vinci, by whom Sodoma was influenced, and the vivid colours of the saint's blue drapery and red cloak, to say nothing of the virtuoso painting of his hand against the Bible, make a vigorously romantic impression.

Appollonio di Giovanni. Cassone front. **The Generosity of Scipio.**

Over door

Jusepe de Ribera (1588-1652). **St. John the Baptist.** The artist was born near Valencia in Spain but worked mostly in Naples, where he died. Richard Buckle writes: "After Caravaggio's introduction of realistic models and dramatic lighting, many Italian artists overlooked spiritual depth for physical beauty in the saints they painted; and this Neapolitan Narcissus is a peasant without a mission in his head".

North wall

On the left, *Carlo Carlone (Lombard, 1686-1776).* **A General receiving the surrender of a city.** The sketch for a big fresco in the Posta d'Acqua (watergate) of the Palazzo Gayyi on the Grand Canal, Venice.

Gaspare Vanvitelli (1647-1736). **Two Roman views.** Vanvitelli was born Dutch but painted in Italy; his son became an Italian architect and built the great palace of Caserta, north of Naples.

Antonio del Pollaiuolo (Florentine, 1432-1498). **Christ at the column.** The picture once belonged to Robert Browning, who mentioned it in his "Old Pictures in Florence":

Could not the ghost with the close red cap, My Pollajolo, the twice a craftsman, Save me a sample, give me the hap of a muscular Christ that shows the draughtsman?

Behind the figure of Christ, St. John the Baptist, St. Jerome with lion and red hat, St. Francis receiving the stigmata, and Tobit with the Angel.

To the right, *Carlo Carlone.* **Minerva as patroness of the Visual Arts.** A preliminary sketch, used for ceilings at both Brühl and Ludwigsburg in Germany.

Gaspare Vanvitelli. **A Roman View.**

Mariotto Albertinelli (Florentine, 1474-1515). **Madonna and Child with St. John the Baptist.**

Above: Pollaiuolo: Christ at the column.

Left: Ribera: St. John the Baptist.

The Dining Room

Above: Chippendale: Urn-topped pedestal.

Bacchus on the chimneypiece.

Below: George Canning by Lawrence.

NOTHING REMAINS OF THE dining room designed by Adam, Barry in the 1840s having raised the ceiling and deepened the room, abolishing at the same time an arched recess (drawings are in the Sir John Soane Museum). To bear witness to Adam's concept, Chippendale's fine dining room chairs remain (with an inch added on to their back legs, presumably to make the diners sit up straighter), and, even more important, at either end of the room the superb **sideboards** and the **urn-topped pedestals** which flank one of them and which rank among the finest English furniture ever made. The urns lined with lead are wine-coolers, while their pedestals conceal silver chests and plate-warmers.

The **Chimneypiece** Adam designed for this room disappeared without trace in Barry's alterations but was replaced by the one designed for the Gallery (by Nollekens, it was once thought). We have now restored the Nollekens (if it was his) to its rightful setting, and in its place stands one which celebrates Bacchus, the patron of food and drink, recently brought from storage and thought to have once stood in a house demolished at some time in the last fifty years. Its style suggests it was carved around 1850 in the manner of a hundred years earlier, which makes it appropriate for Barry's Dining Room. The twelve portraits, with two exceptions, portray owners of Harewood and three of their wives. The only one missing is me, and the first exception is the portrait between the windows and nearest the exit door, of **George Canning** by *Sir Thomas Lawrence P.R.A. (1769-1830)*. The Statesman and Prime Minister is shown in an empty House of Commons, and there are copies of the picture, painted in 1825, at Windsor, Buckingham Palace and in the Foreign Office. The other is over the door by which you entered, of **Edward, Viscount Lascelles,** friend of artists and collector by *John Hoppner (1758-1810)*.

Between the windows, **Edwin Lascelles,** who built Harewood, painted by *Henry Singleton (1766-1839)* in 1795, the year of Edwin's death at well over eighty.

Left of chimneypiece, **Edward, Viscount Lascelles,** by *Hoppner.*

East wall, over sideboard, **Henry, 2nd Earl of Harewood,** by *Lawrence.* The background was painted from a watercolour by Girtin.

West wall, over sideboard, **Henry, 3rd Earl of Harewood** by *Sir Francis Grant P.R.A. (1803-1878)*. He fought at the battle of Waterloo and his Waterloo medal hangs below the relaxed equestrian portrait. Like his father (of whom another likeness hangs to the left of this picture), he was killed by a fall out hunting. On the right-hand side of the fireplace, his wife **Louisa** presides over her new dining room and points proudly at the terrace Barry built for her. *George Richmond (1809-1896)* painted her a few years before she died in 1859.

East wall, over right-hand door, **Henry, 4th Earl of Harewood** by *Sir Edward Poynter P.R.A. (1836-1919)*.

South wall (next to 4th Earl), his son, **Henry, 5th Earl of Harewood** by *Sir William Llewelyn P.R.A. (1863-1941),* wearing the uniform of the Lord Lieutenant and painted in 1916 in his 70th year. His wife **Florence,** my grandmother, hangs over the other door on the same wall by *Solomon J. Solomon,(1860-1927)*.

Over the chimneypiece, **Henry, 6th Earl of Harewood** by *Sir William Nicholson (1872-1949)*. This portrait of my father in the robes of the Order of the Garter was Nicholson's only attempt at a formal state portrait and his biographer records that the search for a compromise between his conscience as a painter and the traditional demands of the undertaking almost drove him to distraction. The portrait of my mother Princess Mary, by *Sir Oswald Birley (1880-1952)* was painted in 1922 as a wedding present for my father from the tenants at Harewood and hangs over the door by which you leave.

Right: Chippendale's sideboard and wine cooler.

45

The Music Room

Terpsichore – the Muse of Dancing. *The eight other Muses, who were companions of Apollo, are depicted in the ceiling panels.*

A TOUR OF HAREWOOD FINISHES WITH the Dining Room, the most completely Victorian room you will see, followed by the Music Room, the one least changed from Adam's concept of well over 200 years ago. There are anachronisms – the Regency console tables on either side of the room and the sofa tables – but by and large the 'overall decorative scheme' at which Adam consistently aimed is not much impaired, and his collaborators are very much to the fore and in their finest form.

See how classically the round ceiling design, mirrored by that of the carpet, fits into the square room! My one regret is that the logistics of getting visitors round the house have suggested the relocation to the Cinnamon Drawing Room of the two pier tables Chippendale designed for the Music Room.

Sèvres porcelain (collected by Edward Lascelles in 1802) is arranged on the console tables, with a late Louis XVI ormolu-mounted striking clock (by *Nicolas Sotiau*) in the middle of the one against the West wall. The ceiling roundels, which depict classical scenes of varying propriety and have been recently cleaned to reveal their pristine colouring, are traditionally thought to be by *Angelica Kaufmann,* and her husband, *Antonio Zucchi* (see page 15 for notes on both), is responsible for the four splendid pictures which grace the walls, seeming, as Richard Buckle said in an earlier guide book, "like windows opening onto views of a half-imaginary Mediterranean". The light from the setting sun reflected on the clouds, not clearly discernible until the pictures were recently cleaned, may have suggested the lilac borders in ceiling and walls.

The chairs and sofas, among Chippendale's grandest, are drawn from two sets, one made for the State Bed and Dressing Rooms, the two bergères taken from the set now in the Yellow Drawing Room and covered, like the chairs and two sofas, in Beauvais tapestry. Chippendale was responsible too for the frame round the picture over the chimneypiece, which is by – who else? – Sir Joshua Reynolds, who emerges somehow as the godfather to a period of style and taste whose creator and presiding genius remains Robert Adam, inspirer of a host of talented collaborators and tickler of the fancy of many a squire. The picture, appropriately if surprisingly, is a family portrait, of Mrs Hale, sister-in-law of the 1st Earl of Harewood, painted as Euphrosyne in Milton's "L'allegro" with some of her children.

"If anyone asks 'Where's the music?' (once wrote Richard Buckle) he must be answered in the words of Keats: 'Heard melodies are sweet, but those unheard are sweeter'. There are lyres woven in the pattern of the carpet, more lyres, pipes and trumpets carved on the marble chimney; and there are ormolu trophies of musical instruments on the magnificent Sèvres clock, which may have belonged to Marie-Antoinette. The central ceiling painting depicts Midas presiding over a musical contest between lyre-playing Apollo and Marsyas, who favoured woodwind. In the Zucchi to the right of the fireplace a band is performing at the top of the stairs; and in his painting on the west wall, there are brigands playing pipes, while a tearful peasant in a red cloak fingers a lute, accompanied with tragic abandon by a lady on the triangle. In the Reynolds portrait group, three of Euphrosyne's children are letting rip on pipe and timpani, while a fourth, deafened by all these painted orchestras, is saying 'Sssh!'".

Above: Reynolds: **Mrs Hale and her children.**

PICTURES

Sir Joshua Reynolds: **Mrs Hale as Euphrosyne (1764).**

Antonio Zucchi: **An Italian Seaport, with Roman temple and statue of Neptune. A palatial courtyard open to the sky. The ruins of Dalmatia. An Italian Fair, with a dentist.**

Below: Zucchi: **The ruins of Dalmatia.**

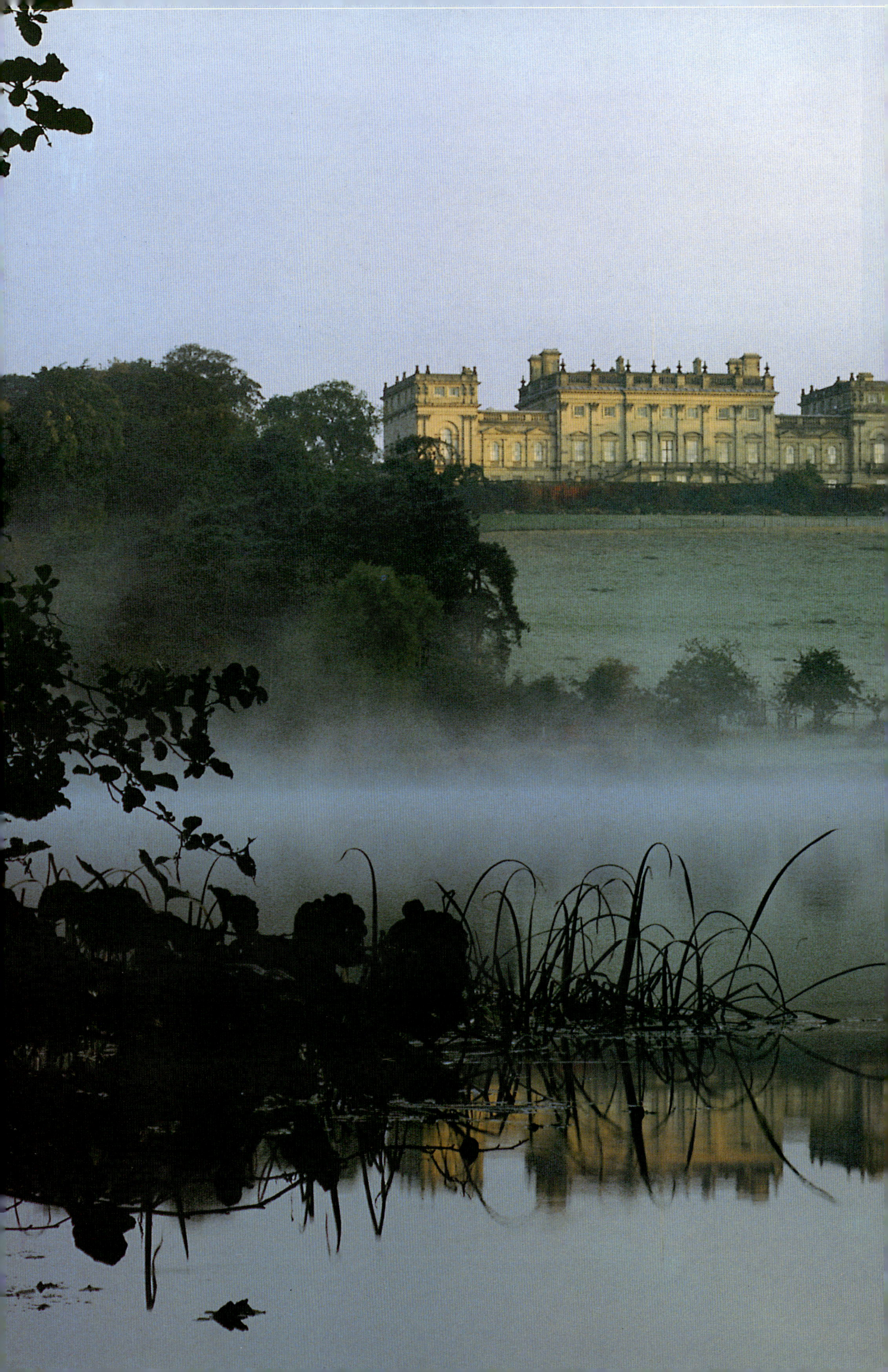

Music at Harewood

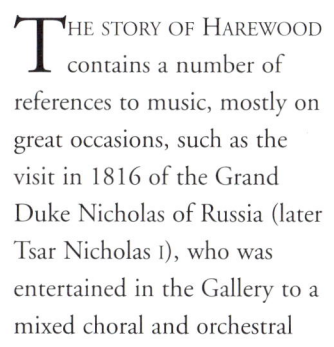

The winter season Gallery Concerts at Harewood play host to numerous national and international artists.

The story of Harewood contains a number of references to music, mostly on great occasions, such as the visit in 1816 of the Grand Duke Nicholas of Russia (later Tsar Nicholas I), who was entertained in the Gallery to a mixed choral and orchestral programme of music mainly by Handel and Haydn. The mind boggles at the torrent of sound which must have been released in the Hallelujah Chorus, which was one of the Handel pieces. The Grand Duke's host, the 1st Earl, was a keen patron of music, and his account book records sums for the tuning of his instruments, the purchase of a violin, and payment to singers and instrumentalists. In my grandfather's time, an organ was added to the stock of furniture, and early in the Second World War, when the house was a hospital, Sadler's Wells Opera (during a stint at the Grand Theatre in Leeds) came to perform Mozart's *The Marriage of Figaro* on an improvised stage at the south end of the Gallery.

In the late 1960s my wife and I decided to institute a regular winter series of chamber concerts to take place in the Gallery, which has almost ideal ambience and acoustics for music on this scale. We started the series with recitals by the great Bulgarian bass, Boris Christoff, and the Janáček string quartet from Czechoslovakia, the latter appearing only a few weeks after the infamous invasion of their country and the fall of Dubček, so that their playing of music by the composer from whom they took their name had such fire and conviction as to seem like a manifesto, a declaration of faith in the future of a world which had turned against them. Great performers like the pianist Alfred Brendel, the Chilingirian string quartet and the horn player Barry Tuckwell have been regular contributors to the series.

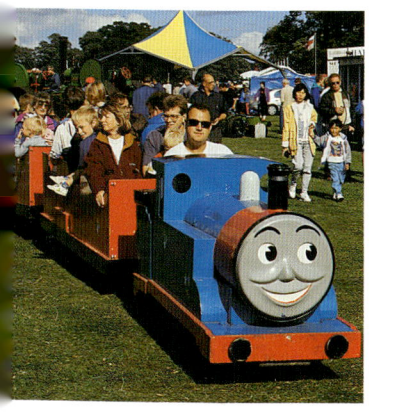

Events and Education

Special events feature regularly in the Harewood calendar.

Country houses like Harewood have over the centuries acted as host to numerous events – country shows, steam rallies, dog trials, craft fairs, cricket matches, horse shows, outdoor concerts, car rallies, conferences, corporate dinners and the like. Harewood is no exception, with a busy programme throughout the year.

Education plays a role at Harewood and thousands of children have learned from our award-winning Education Department at first hand about conservation and the countryside. We now also run workshops with artists exhibiting in the Terrace Gallery, and plan to develop adult education with specialist tours and lectures in the near future.

Designed and produced by:
Andrew Esson, Designers and Partners Ltd., Oxford.
Design consultancy by:
Diane Lascelles.
Photography by:
Clare Arron, Richard Davies, Richard Dixon, Nigel Judge, Jim Kershaw, Charlie Nickols, Hugh Palmer, Terry Suthers and Ken Ward.
Printed and finished by:
Raithby Lawrence, Leicester.

ACKNOWLEDGEMENTS

John Jewell: *The History and Antiquities of Harewood in Yorkshire* (1819); John Jones: *History and Antiquities of Harewood* (1850); Tancred Borenius: *The Harewood Collection - Pictures* (Oxford University Press, 1936); Hugh Tait: *Sèvres Porcelain in the collection of the Earl of Harewood* (Apollo magazine: June 1964, January 1965, June 1966); Richard Buckle: *Harewood. A Guide Book* (1959: 1962); Dorothy Stroud: *Capability Brown* (1975); Mary Mauchline: *Harewood House* (revised 1992); Christopher Gilbert: *The Life and Work of Thomas Chippendale* (Studio Vista - Christie's 1972).

Harewood Today

I OFTEN WONDER WHAT EDWIN Lascelles would think of Harewood today. Quite apart from the architectural alterations to the House and its surroundings, would it all seem very strange to him? Or would he see a Harewood that is moving forward, very much alive and kicking, into the 21st century as somewhere that he recognises, a continuation and a vindication of the work he had started more than 200 years earlier?

We often use the word "continuum" when talking about what we're trying to achieve here. By this we mean that, although we are keenly aware of Harewood's history, we do not see our role as being simply to preserve that history in aspic, but to deal with the present and look to the future with the same spirit of enterprise and sense of excellence that was in action when Harewood was first built.

For example: although it might seem that much of the work here is to do with conservation – of buildings, of paintings and furniture, of landscape and gardens – we are also very much involved in new enterprises. Harewood supports contemporary artists as well as showing the work of the past. Harewood is about finding new uses for old buildings as well as looking after its architectural heritage. Everything we do has to mean something now, be significant today – not just for the people who live or work here but also for the many thousands who visit and enjoy the House and Grounds every year.

So Harewood must continue to re-invent itself. The House is now run as a charitable trust, able to attract public funds from English Heritage and the European Community, one of the first privately-run stately homes in Britain to achieve museum status. These are just the means, however. The end is something more ambitious: not simply to look after a beautiful and tranquil piece of England but to make sure it continues to be somewhere truly alive and exciting and modern, looking forward with eagerness as well as looking back with respect.

David Lascelles

The Bird Garden

Top left: Waldrapp Ibis.
Top right: Bali Starling.
Above: Pink Pigeon.

Below: Twilight over the lake.

As you stand on the Terrace looking towards the Lake, you will see the Old Stables to your right at the bottom of the hill. Built by John Carr in the 1750s just before the House, today they house a restaurant, shops, education centre and conference facilities. Through them you now also enter the Bird Garden.

The Bird Garden was opened in 1970, and stands on a sloping 4-acre site between Stables and Lake. Every attempt has been made to make it seem part of Capability Brown's landscape, but it nonetheless provides a home to some 120 species of exotic, non-British birds, a third of which are considered vulnerable or endangered in their native habitat. It comprises over 40 aviaries (built of wood and local stone) and a range of open enclosures. The Lake itself is home to a variety of birds, including a flock of Chilean flamingoes, as well as migratory species.

At Harewood, we have always tried to show extraordinary birds from around the world in the context of a beautiful landscape. But at the same time we try to engage fully with key contemporary conservation issues. Our membership of the Federation of Zoological Gardens of Great Britain and Northern Ireland means that we are part of a number of captive breeding programmes, and many of the birds on display have been bred at Harewood. We have strong links with the World Pheasant Association, with a number of aviaries dedicated to breeding the more endangered varieties of these magnificent birds – such as the extremely rare Palawan Peacock Pheasant.

Our Curator, Jim Irwin-Davis, and his staff are regularly successful in breeding other endangered species, birds like the Mauritius Pink Pigeon which was down to a mere 33 birds in the wild until Gerald Durrell captured 11 of them and set up breeding programmes in Jersey and Mauritius.

The Bird Garden has contributed to overseas expeditions and been the venue for numerous conferences and symposiums.

Beneath the bridge and the waterfall at the West end of the lake, the rock garden hosts a spectacular variety of colour in the spring and summer months.

The Gardens and Lakeside Walk

GARDENS HAVE A tendency to evolve, and a walk from the house down to the Stables reveals what changing tastes and needs have suggested: shrubs to replace the tall trees which blew down in 1962 and left an open rather than a canopied area, and a screen of evergreen hedges to shield garden-lovers from those using the road. The first version of the **Adventure Playground** was opened in 1970 by the footballer Jack Charlton, and its successor in 1993 by another Leeds United and England footballer, Tony Dorigo. Its resemblance in summer to an animated ant-heap testifies to its popularity. The **Stables** at the bottom of the hill was the first aspect of John Carr's extensive work at Harewood to be completed.

The **Lakeside walk** suggests a passion on the part of Harewood's owners for the Rhododendron, a phenomenon new to English gardens in the nineteenth century, and it is true that my parents shared a very strong interest in the species, subscribing to pre-war expeditions to the Himalayas. I think it would be very much to their taste that all named species at Harewood are now recorded on computer disk. A print-out is available on request at the Estate Office (near the Lodge), together with a map showing individual locations.

Gunnera (top left and right), and Rhododendrons (top right and bottom left).

John Sparrow was the Head Gardener who was charged with damming the stream to make a **lake,** some years before Lancelot Brown pronounced on the 'capabilities' of the landscape, and the dam is a feature of the walk round the lake to the kitchen gardens. The waterfall which joins lake to outgoing stream dominates the rocky garden below the dam, which spectacularly celebrates spring each year, with a profusion of primulas, astilbes, hosta, and the water-loving gunnera, a member of the rhubarb family which grows to eight or nine feet each summer before subsiding with the first frosts to provide a dingy mulch for the plant's resurrection the following year.

removed from Clumber, were added by my father in 1937. Four little marble statues on the seats at either end of the Terrace are by *Pieter von Baurscheit the younger,* dated 1725, and on the Upper Terrace there is a further group dated 1729. Orpheus with a leopard by *Astrid Zydower* (born 1930) adorns the central fountain, taking the place of Barry's original which disintegrated as a result of frost in 1982.

The Dolphin Garden, which is a feature of the West end of the Upper Terrace, was suggested by an idea of David Hicks, with terracotta dolphins in the centre and a French terracotta figure of Autumn at the end of the vista to the West.

THE TERRACE GALLERY

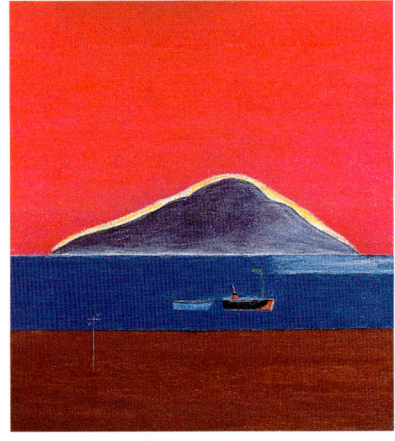

What was the Sub Hall in Carr's and Adam's original scheme, situated beneath the Library on the south side of the house, was refurbished in 1989 specifically for use as an art gallery. It opened with an exhibition of contemporary works in aid of Survival International entitled **Images of Paradise,** and since then a changing programme of contemporary art has been shown each year. Notably in 1992 a major exhibition of Australian Aboriginal Art was followed by a Sidney Nolan retrospective. In 1993 the programme included Andy Goldsworthy and an exhibition of contemporary furniture makers, complementing the Chippendale in the House. 1994 featured three Scottish artists – Ron O'Donnell, Barbara Rae and Craigie Aitchison.

Holy Island from Lamlash, 1994, by Craigie Aitchison (lent from a private collection).

The Terrace

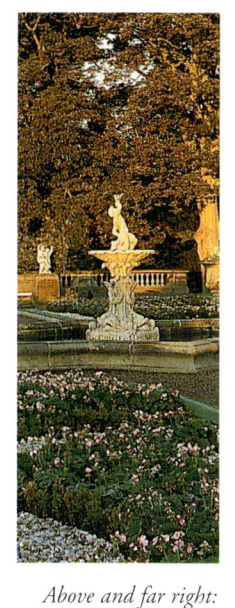

Above and far right: Fountain by Raymond Smith, c.1850.

Below: Barry's Terrace restored and newly planted, 1994.

Visitors to Harewood will have noticed two things early on – the stretch of grass before the front door on the North side, and the view of the lake over the Terrace on the South – and think they were well calculated. Yet, curiously, this was not quite the case. The North front for 200 years looked onto a rough field in which cattle and deer grazed, and it was the exigencies of opening the house to the public which suggested something a little smoother so that the grass is now regularly mown.

The Terrace was added only in mid-nineteenth century and before that the South door, like that of many 18th century houses, gave onto a grass field. Within a few years of inheriting Harewood from his father in 1841, Henry, 3rd Earl of Harewood and his wife Louisa commissioned *Sir Charles Barry (1795-1860)* to transform the House and its setting. The plan for the Terrace, on two levels, was put into action in the 1840s, and by 1861 Roger Fenton's photographs show Terrace and parterre in very much the form to which they were, in 1994, restored (with invaluable assistance from the EC and from English Heritage) – restoration master-minded and directed by Harewood's Head Gardener, Michael Walker. The original design went through a number of stages but the final concept was as it is today. Dwarf box hedges contain the patterns within which flowers bring colour to the scheme. Yew was used to give height but the urns,

The Grounds and Gardens

IF MAN PROPOSES, as over landscape in eighteenth century England he most certainly started to, all sorts of factors terrestrial and divine immediately start to dispose. Like Robert Adam, Capability Brown and Humphry Repton planned to dazzle the eyes of the squire, but as soon as earth-shifting and treeplanting were complete, change and decay inexorably took over. Trees grew up and flourished, sometimes obscured what the planners intended to be visible, in their turn blew down and were either replaced (thus avoiding decay) or were simply carted off with the resultant clearing maybe more to later taste than what Brown or Repton had plotted (thus ensuring change).

At Harewood, the view from the House is still dominated by what the great eighteenth century landscape architects planned, and we continue to plant in the shapes documented by contemporary descriptions or recorded by painters (no plans survive). How well those shapes accommodate Barry's Terrace or our twentieth century Bird Garden only the visitor, armed with a modern sense of evolution, can decide.